NAME

a cow got on a rock

a cow got on a rock

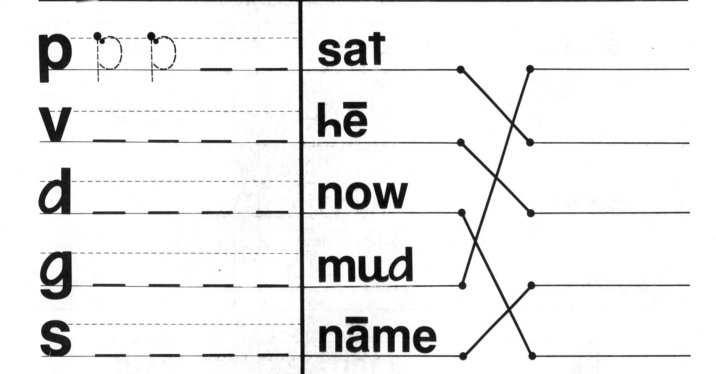

p p p	sat	
v	hē	
d	now	
g	mud	
s	nāme	

on man man said ~~man~~

man not

man sand

man shāve man

man sō

rock mad man

man nēēd

shack

ēars

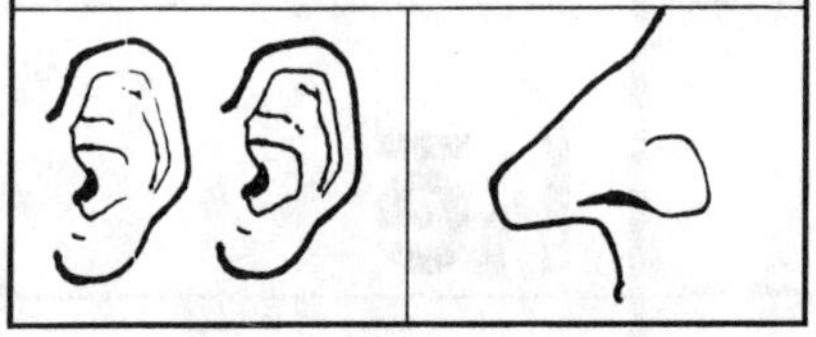

hut

a fish

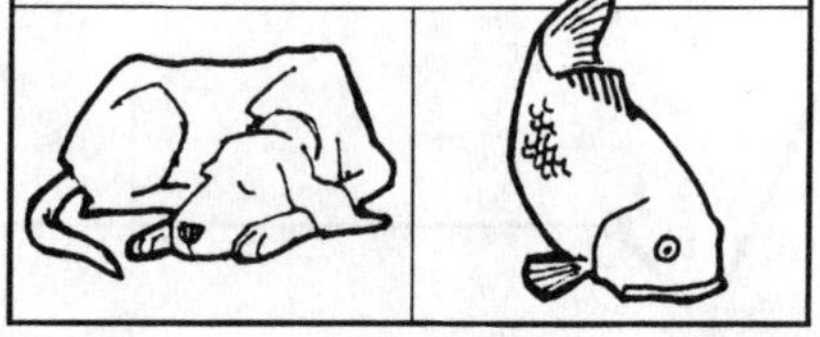

him

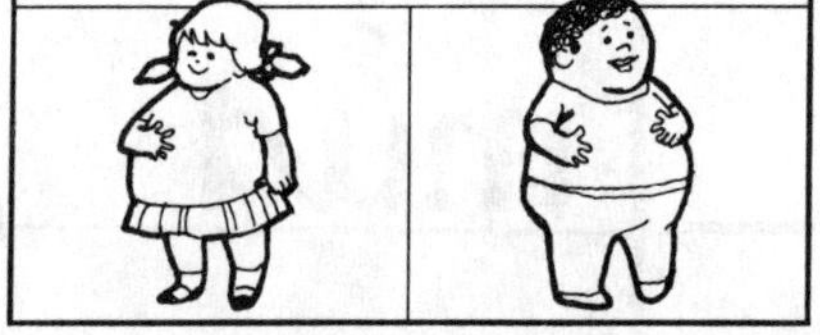

ōld

lāke

a mitt

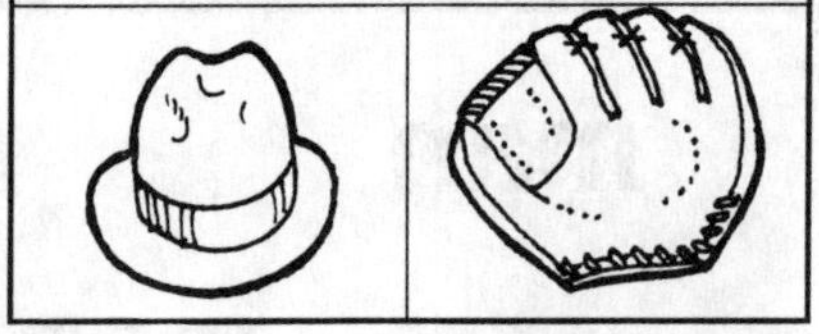

a sack

mom

fēēt

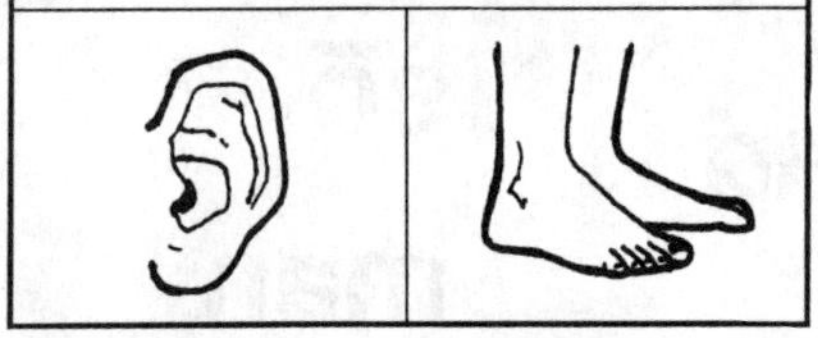

a cow

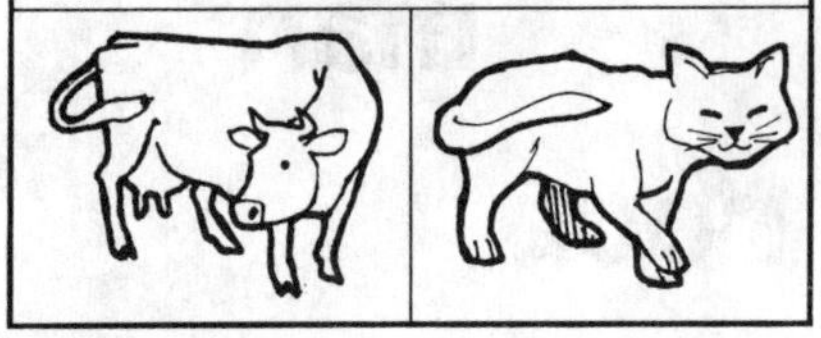

Printed in the United States of America.

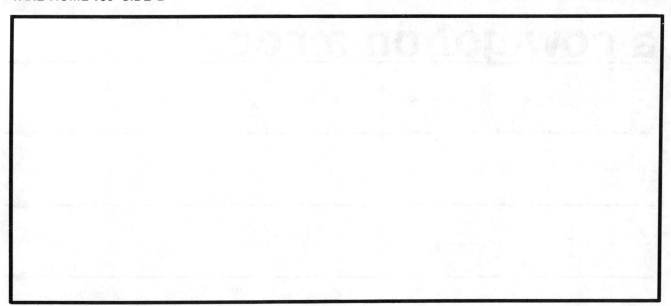

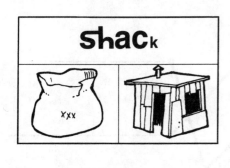

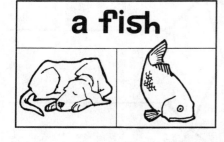

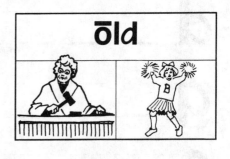

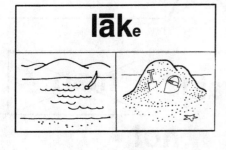

hē had sand on him.

hē had sand on him.

p p p _ _	sock
g _ _ _ _	of
v _ _ _ _	run
t _ _ _ _	ham
I _ _ _	to

~~sand~~

now sand and sand on sand gāve sand sand ōld little sand sand sand sat fēēt sand gō

a cōat

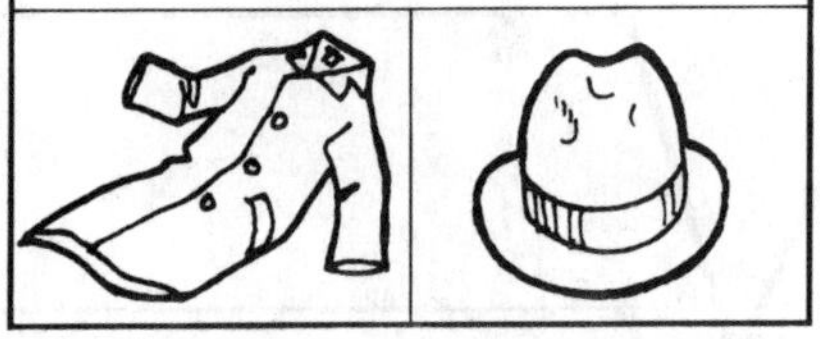

hill

lock

a tāil

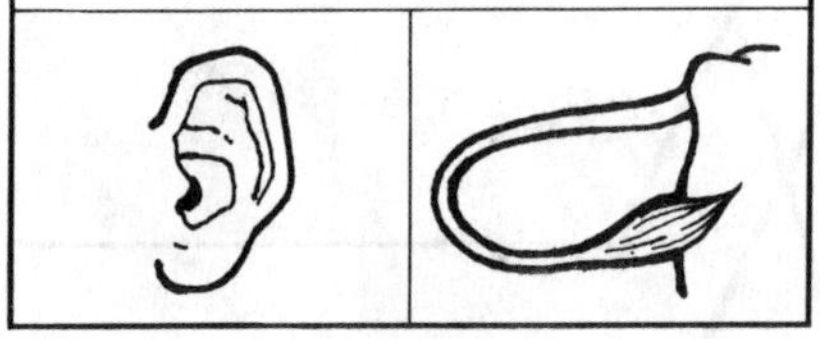

tēēth

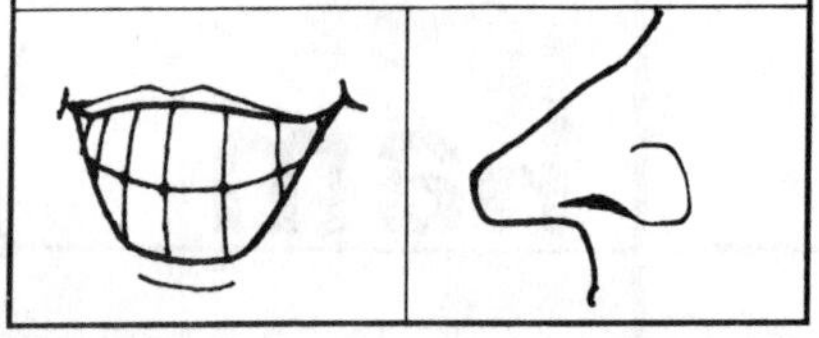

a dish

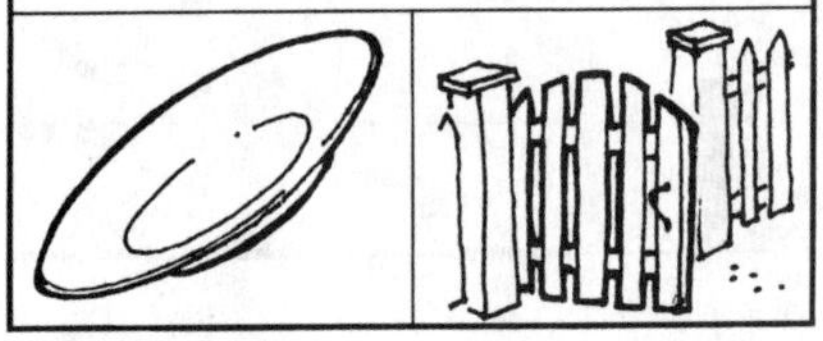

nōse

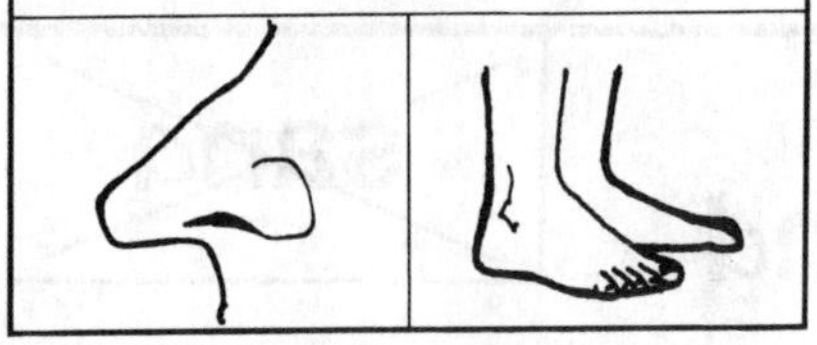

hut

gōat

shē

a rāke

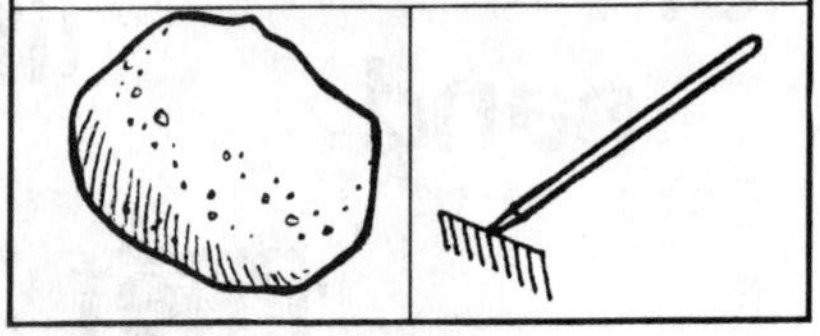

cōld

Printed in the United States of America.

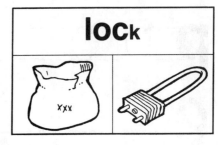

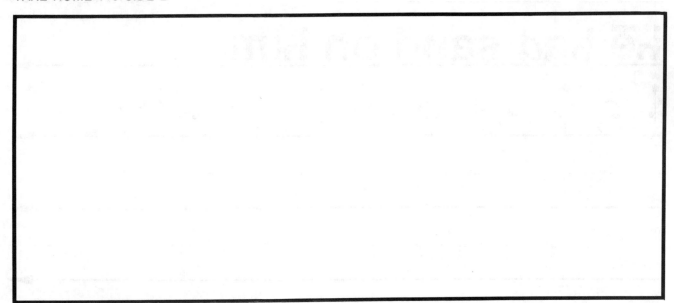

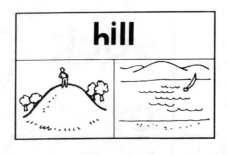

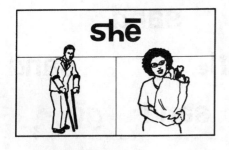

thē fat man and his fat cow
got on a little rock.

a cat said, "fat man, that rock
will not hōld a fat man and his
cow. that rock will gō down
thē hill."

did thē rock gō down thē hill
with thē fat man and his fat
cow?

Printed in the United States of America.

NAME ______________________________

hē ran thē fan.

hē ran thē fan.

sh ___ ___	cow
th ___ ___	did
o ___ ___ ___ ___	lock
ō ___ ___ ___ ___	ēat
v ___ ___ ___ ___	mom

~~run~~

run sō run run

run is fun run

lāte run rag

run run

run got rug

sand did

gōat

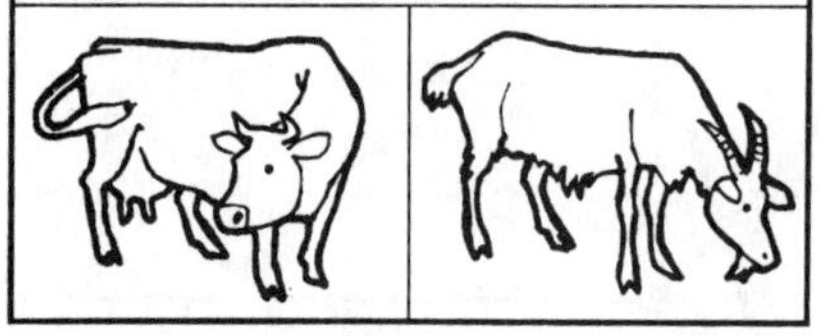

man

māil

fish

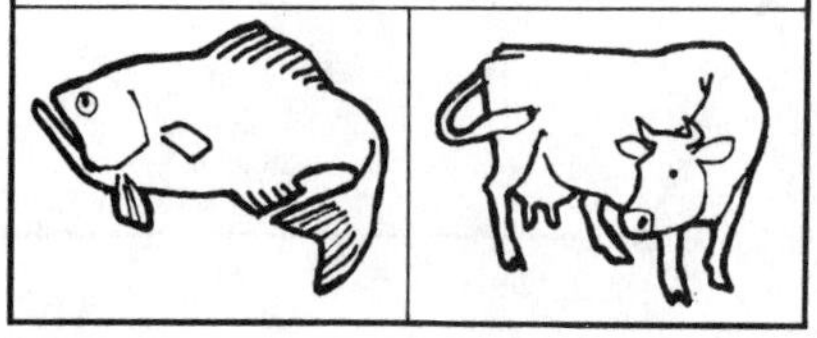

cōld

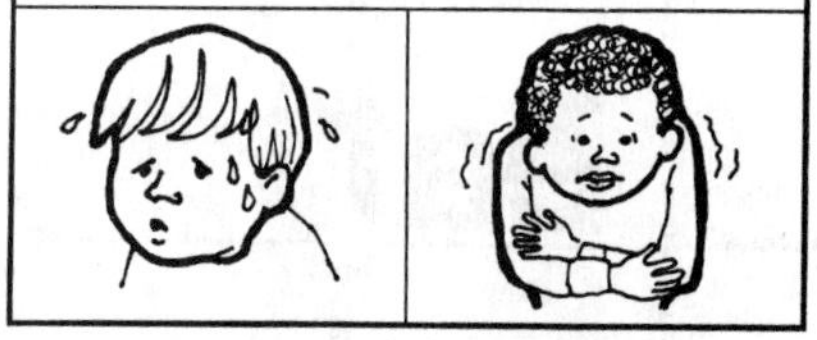

kitten

a rāke

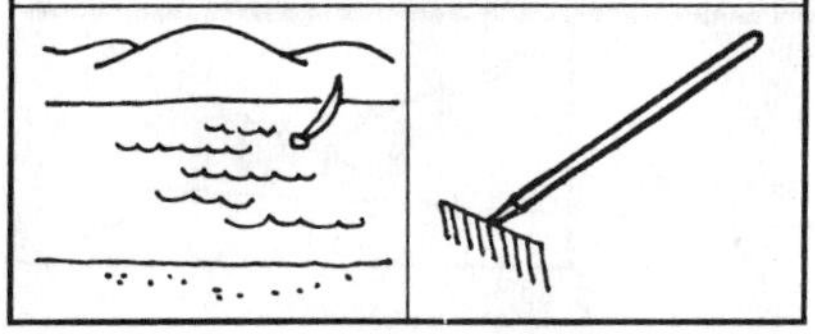

kiss

fēet

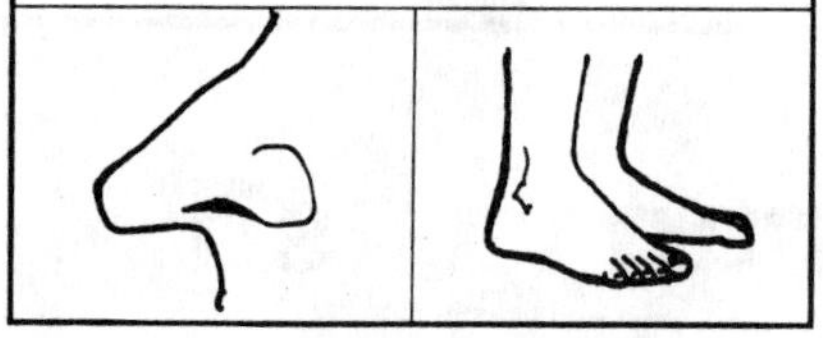

a shack

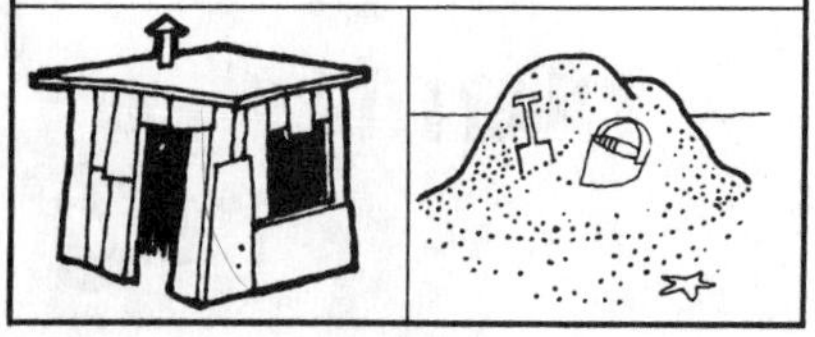

a fan

ēars

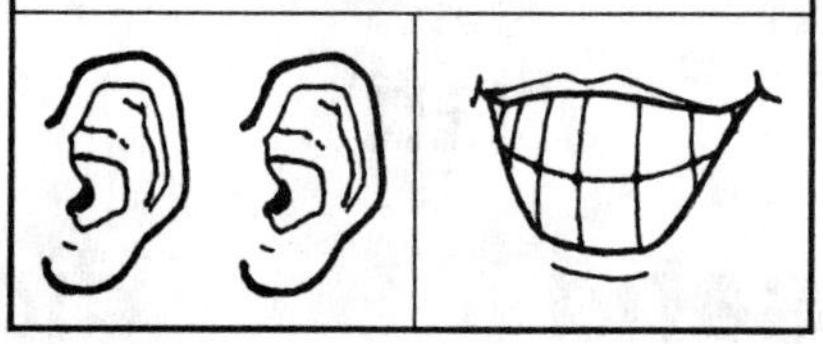

Printed in the United States of America.

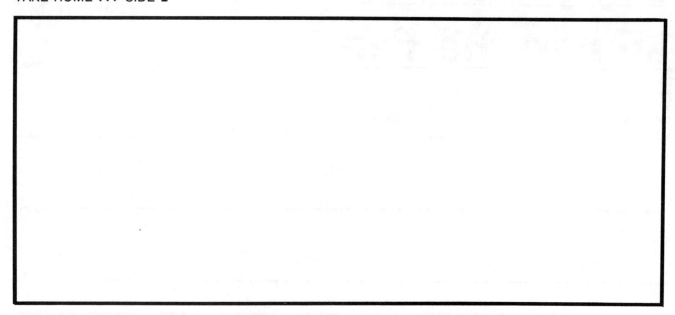

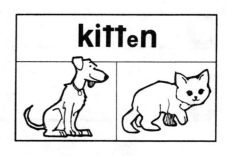

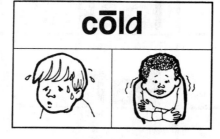

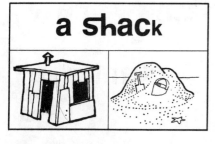

thē dog āte thē car.

thē dog āte thē car.

r _ _ _ _	fun
sh _ _ _	give
ē _ _ _ _	māde
u _ _ _ _	lick
l _ _ _ _	and

~~hand~~

sand
hand
hand
sit
hat
cow
hand
hand
cōld
hand
hand
hot
hand
hand
hand
nēēd
and
hand
was

thē cōats

cow

cōld

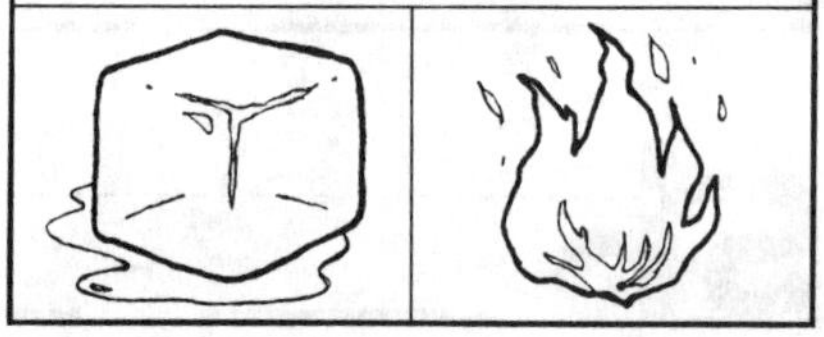

mitt

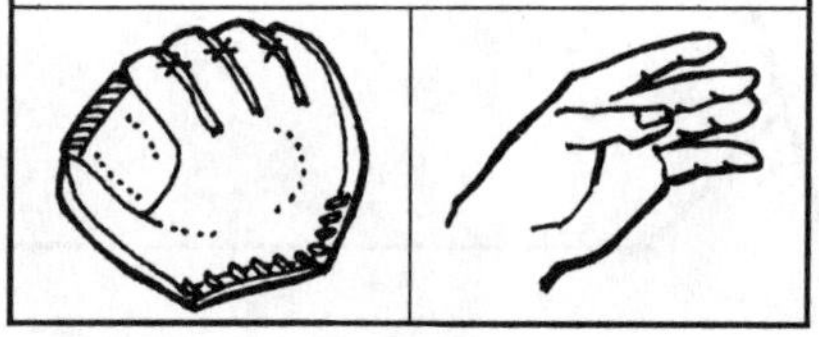

a nōse

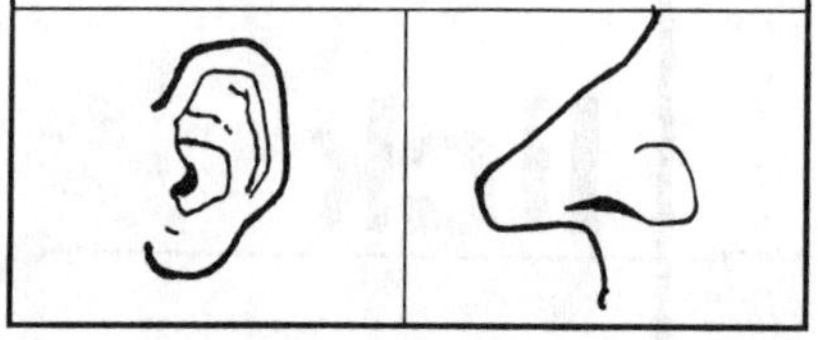

gāte

a rāke

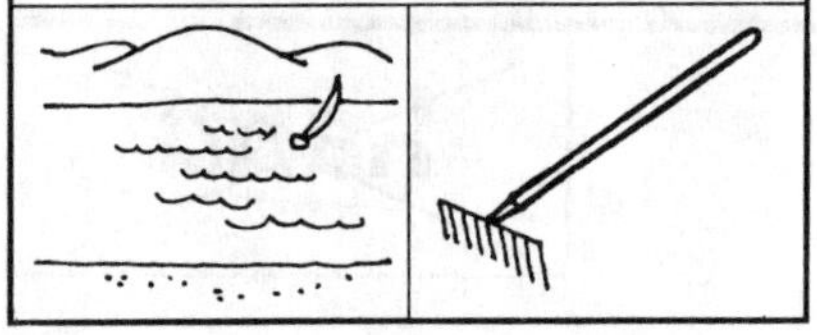

socks

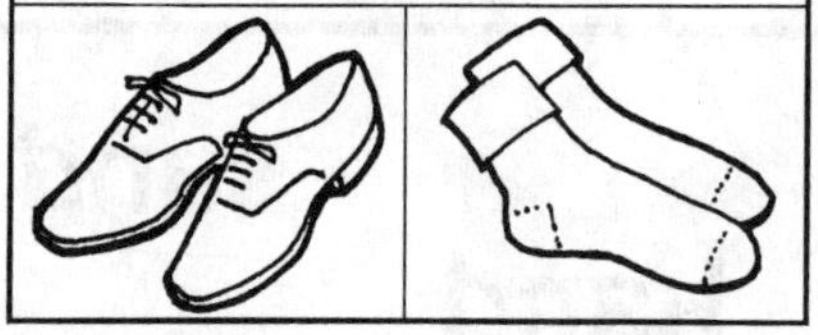

a rug

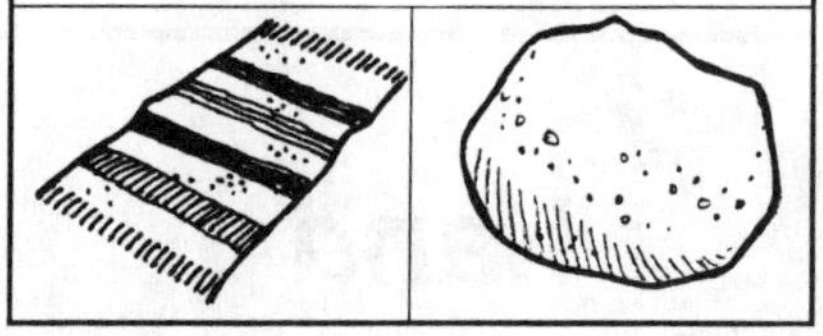

sack

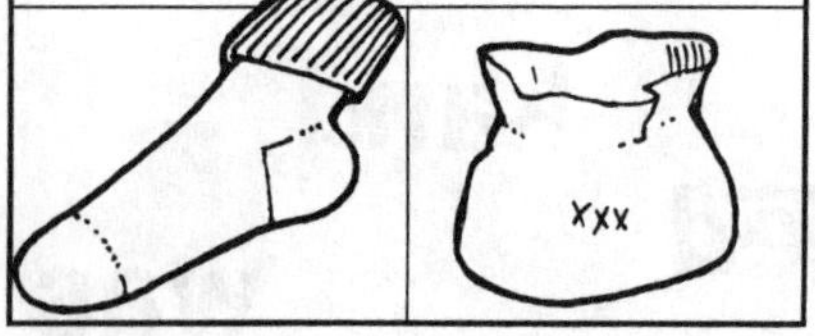

hē

a lāke

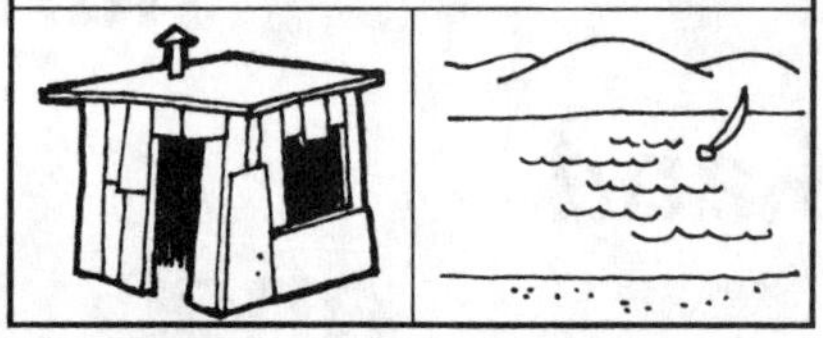

Printed in the United States of America.

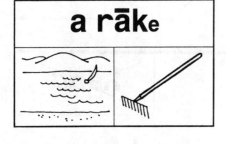

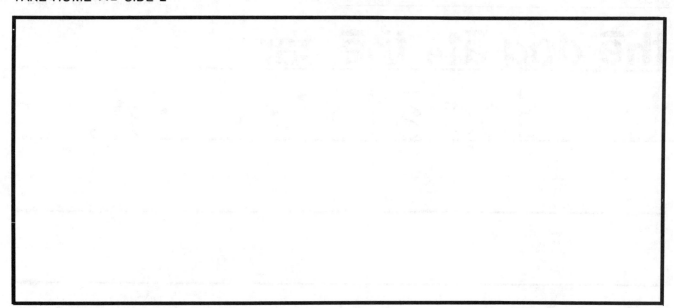

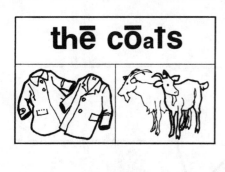

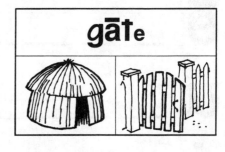

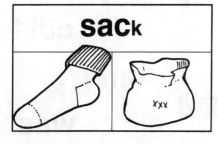

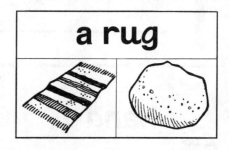

thē gōat sat on a log.

the goat sat on a log.

p p p _ _	tāil
c _ _ _ _	rāke
f _ _ _ _	cōld
ā _ _ _ _	is
v _ _ _ _	sock

~~dog~~

dog log dog did

gāte dog nō dog dog

dog said

dish dog shāve dog

dog cow hē

rock

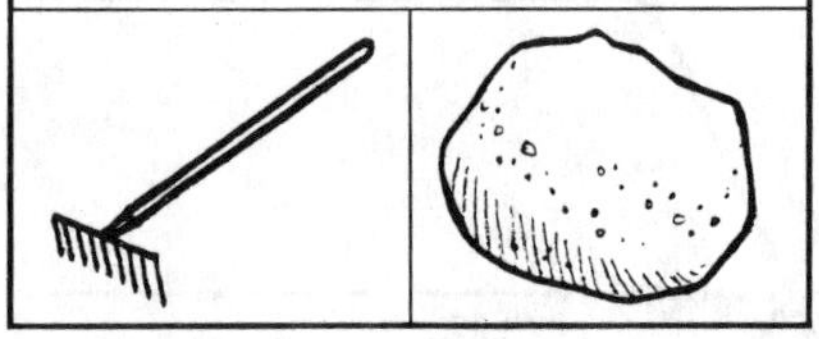

sand

a cow

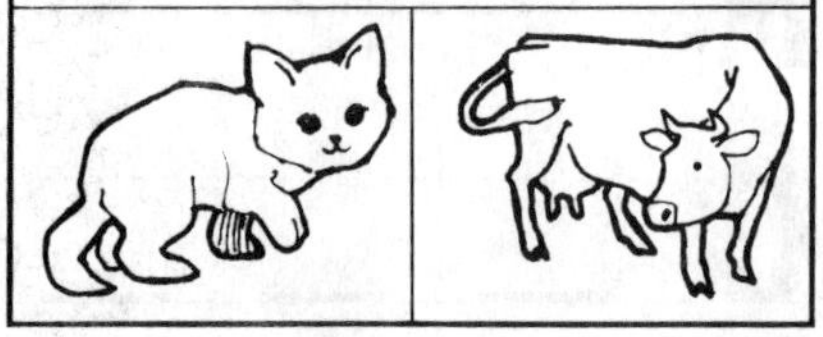

tēēth

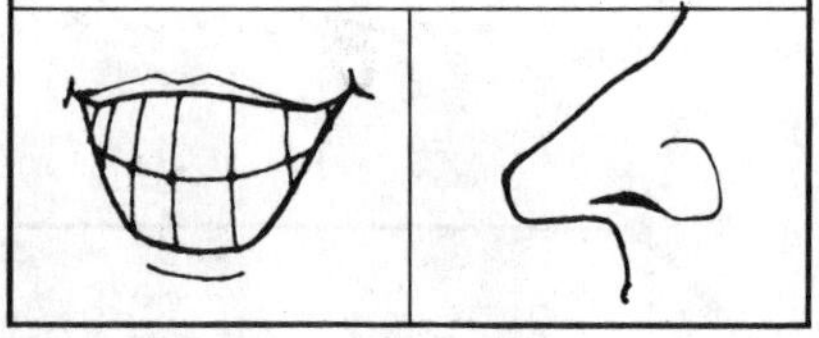

sun

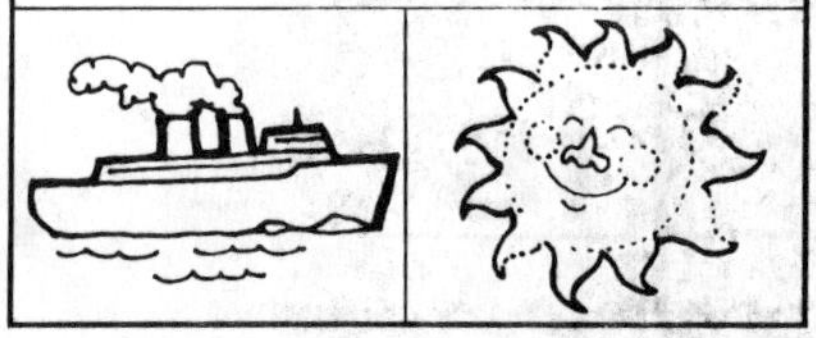

mom

socks

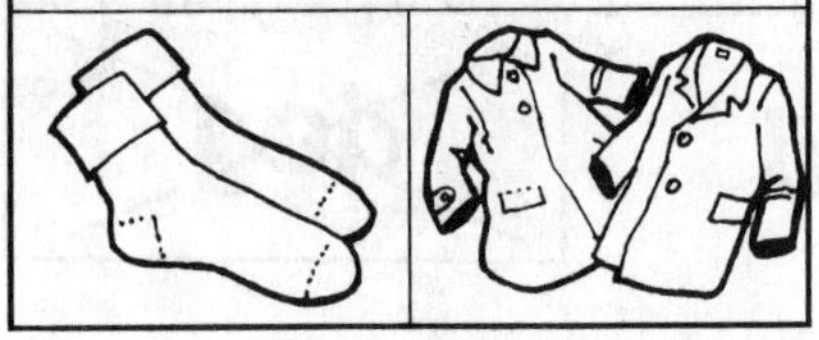

a cōat

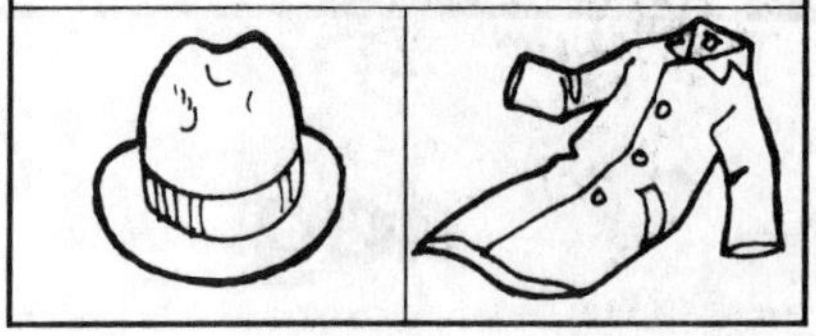

ēars

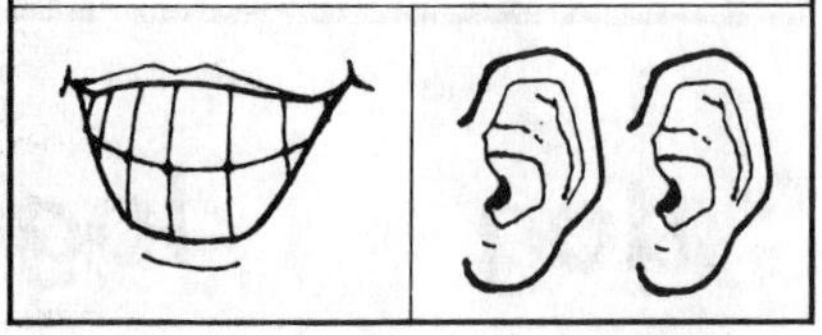

tāil

hill

a gōat

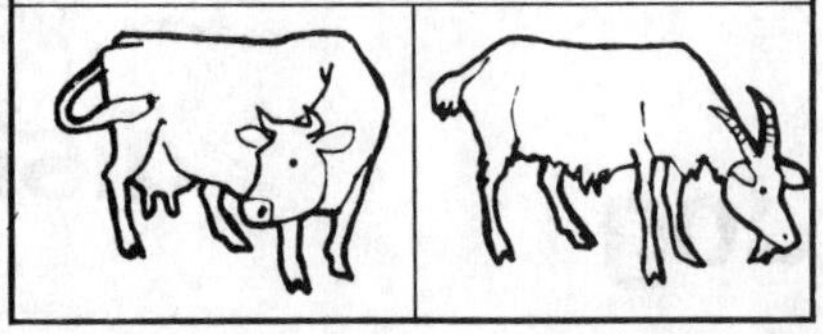

Printed in the United States of America.

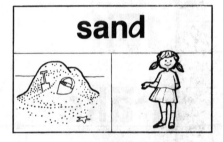

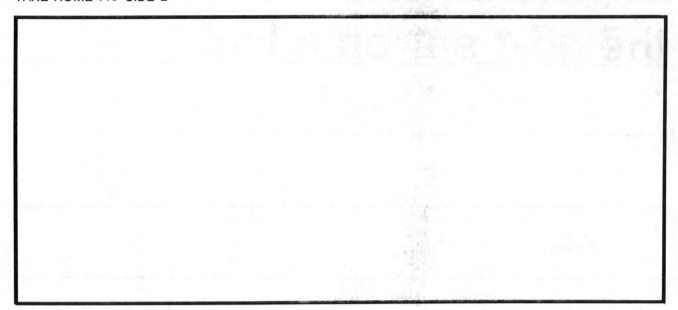

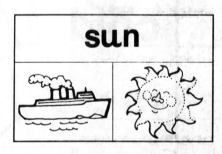

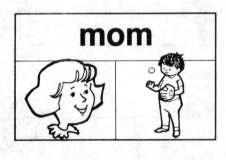

a man sat on a gōat.

a man sat on a gōat.

l _ _ _ _	ēars
i _ _ _ _	gōat
w _ _ _	sō
ch ch ch	sad
v _ _ _ _	hē

~~pot~~

his farm pot
pot
pot
pot
shē pot
pot got
pot
fōr cop top pot
pot
said sō

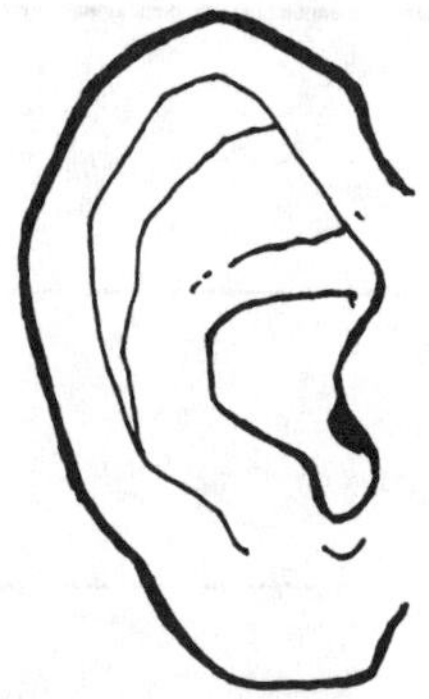

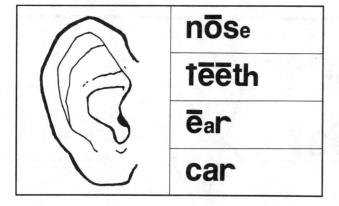

nōse
tēēth
ēar
car

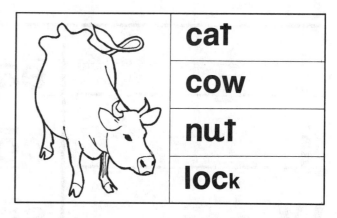

cat
cow
nut
lock

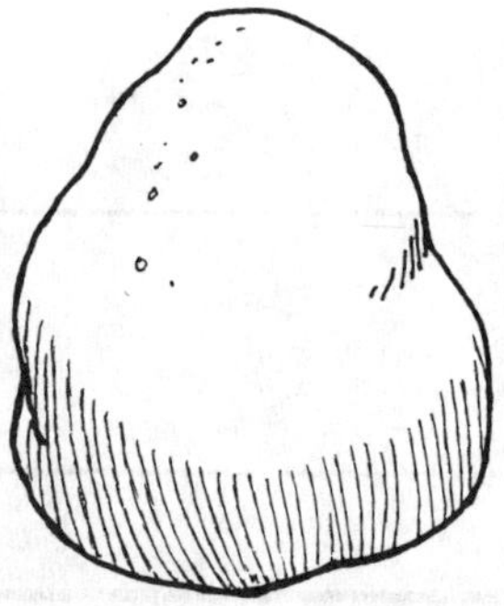

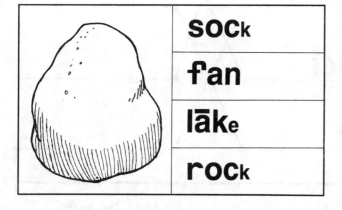

sock
fan
lāke
rock

rat
fish
rāke
hut

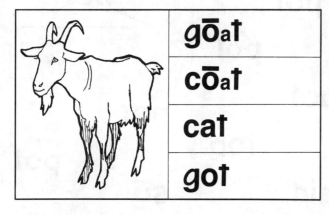

gōat
cōat
cat
got

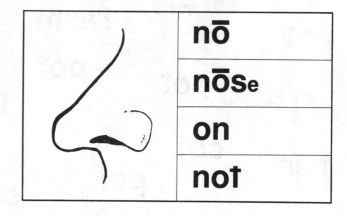

nō
nōse
on
not

Printed in the United States of America.

NAME ____________________

hē has lots of cars.

hē has lots of cars.

ch ch ch	fat	
i _ _ _ _	hill	
w _ _ _	not	
h _ _ _ _	said	
m _ _ _	ran	

~~fish~~

is fish was fish

fish fish thē

fat fish

wish am fish

fog fish

fish

now fish lāte

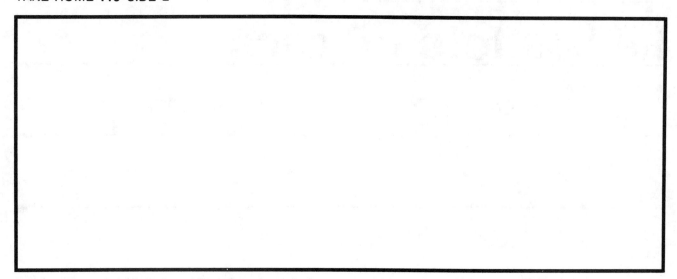

man
cat
tāil
car

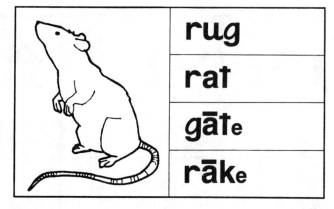

rug
rat
gāte
rāke

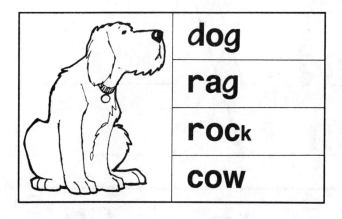

dog
rag
rock
cow

log
dish
shack
gōat

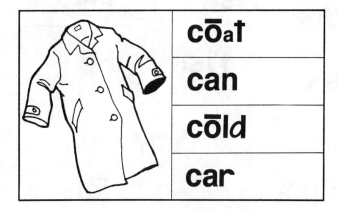

cōat
can
cōld
car

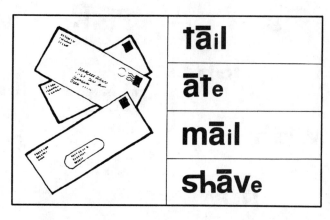

tāil
āte
māil
shāve

Printed in the United States of America.

shē said, "I have a fan."

hē said, "I have sand."

shē said, "wē can run thē sand in thē fan." sō hē ran thē fan nēar thē sand.

hē had sand in his ēars. hē said, "I can not hēar."

hē had sand on his sēat. shē said, "wē have sand on us."

Printed in the United States of America.

thē dog said, "nō."

thē dog said, "nō."

ā	have
ch ch ch	sand
d	thē
g	him
p	lāke

girl

girl if said sack girl log

girl not girl sō girl

girl girl girl gōat fēēt girl sand

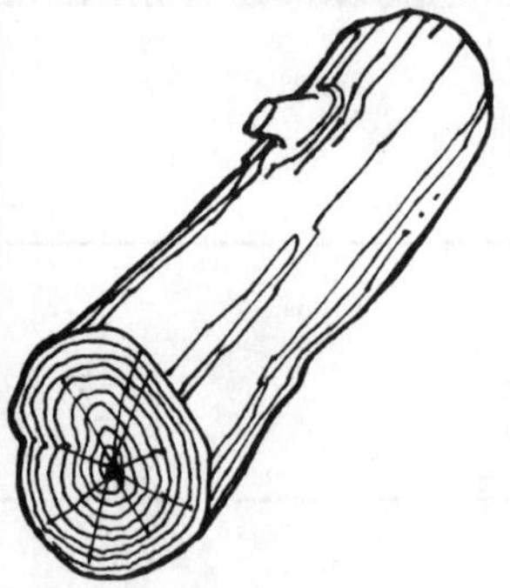

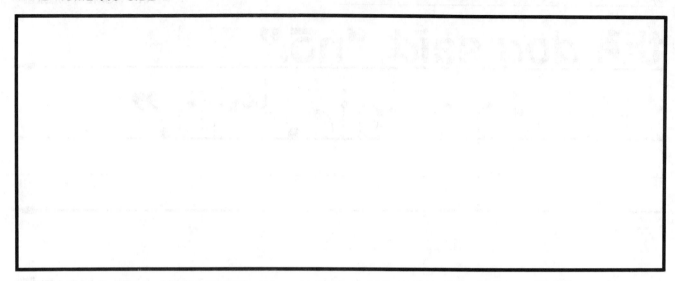

nōse	
fan	
log	
cow	

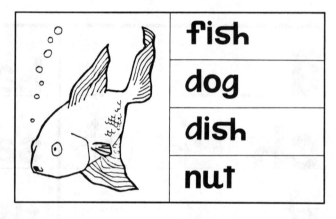

fish	
dog	
dish	
nut	

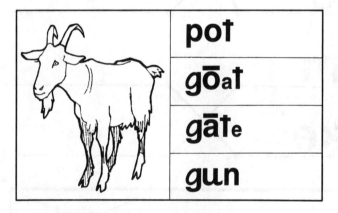

pot	
gōat	
gāte	
gun	

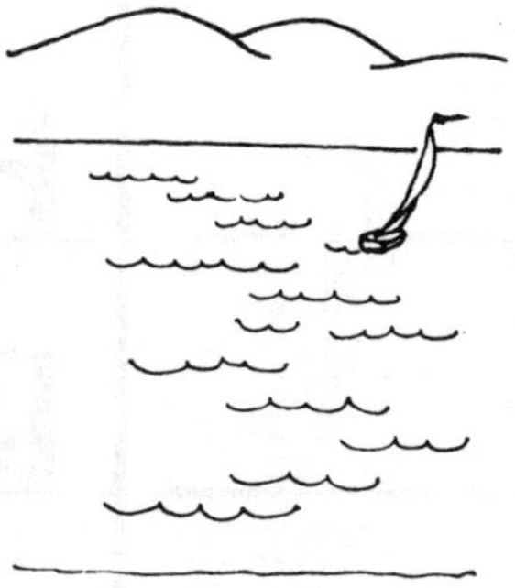

tāil	
rock	
lāke	
sack	

sad	
sand	
and	
fan	

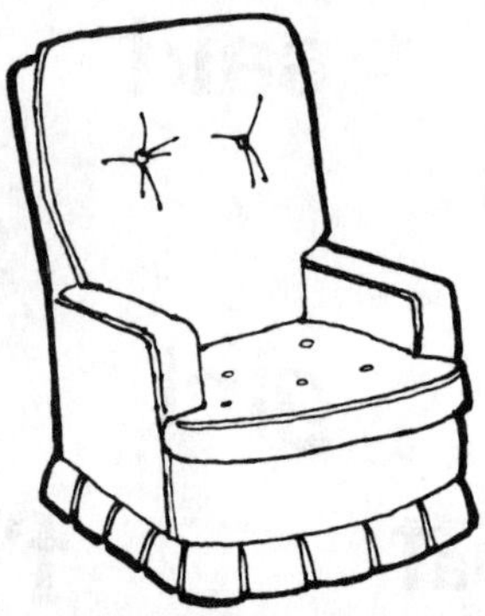

sēat	
fēēt	
shē	
said	

Printed in the United States of America.

a girl was in a cāve.

a girl was in a cāve.

s ___ ___ ___ ___	rock
ch ___ ___	mē
f ___ ___ ___ ___	dog
v ___ ___ ___ ___	it
p ___ ___ ___ ___	cow

~~farm~~

gōat sit farm hand farm farm said farm farm hē farm farm farm ōld farm little run now

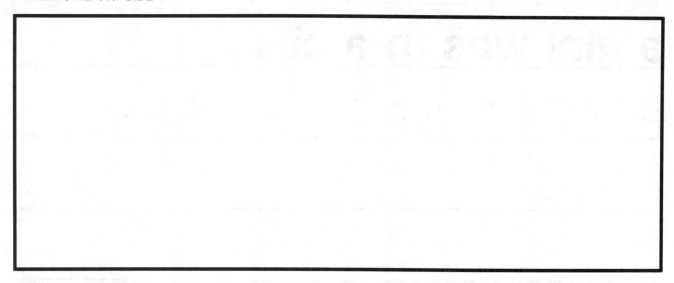

- hē
- fish
- man
- shē

- mad
- fat
- sad
- mēan

- lock
- cōat
- sack
- hut

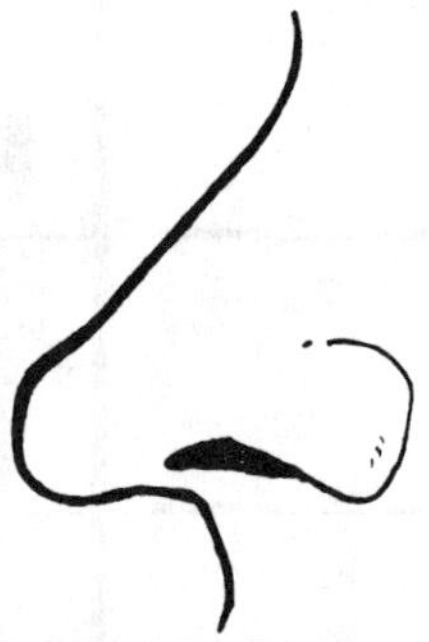

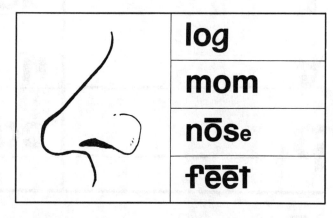

- log
- mom
- nōse
- fēēt

- ran
- rōad
- dog
- car

- āte
- rock
- gāte
- fish

Printed in the United States of America.

hē has lots of pots.

hē has lots of pots.

o _ _ _ _	pot
v _ _ _ _	nāme
sh _ _	kiss
w _ _ _	tar
a _ _ _ _	hut

~~cars~~

cars cars will

had

was cars

cars cars

cars

fish cars

cars how cars

nō cars āte car is

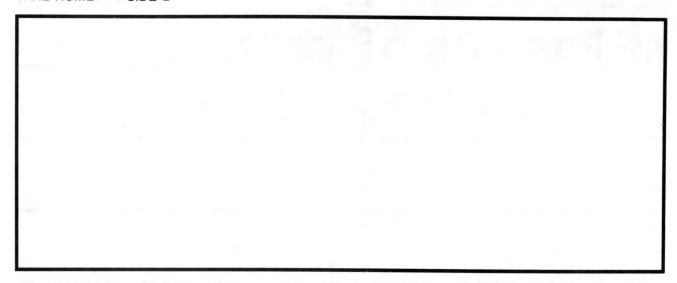

hat
cōat
rug
dog

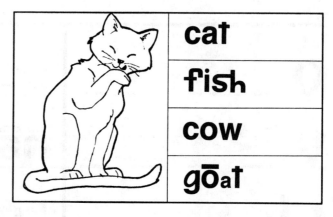

cat
fish
cow
gōat

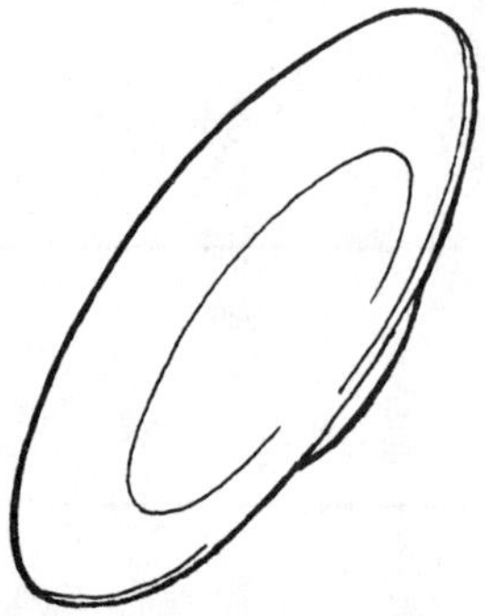

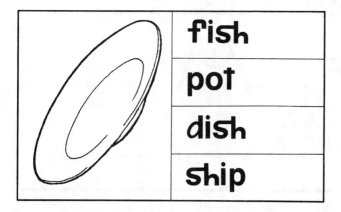

fish
pot
dish
ship

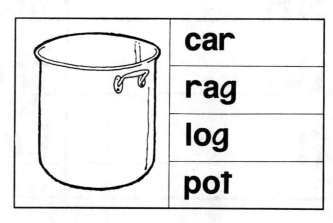

car
rag
log
pot

fat
cow
car
farm

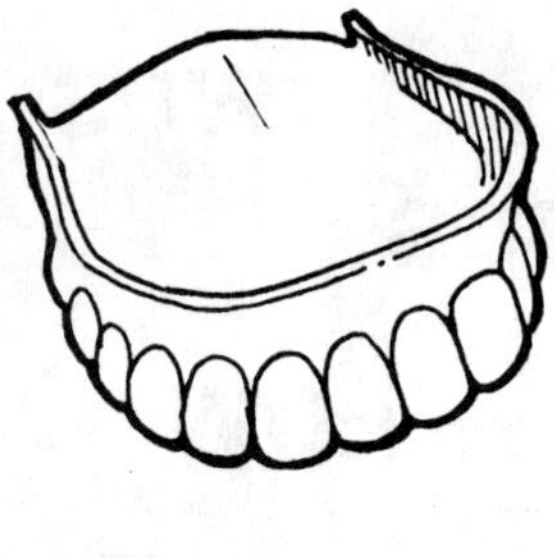

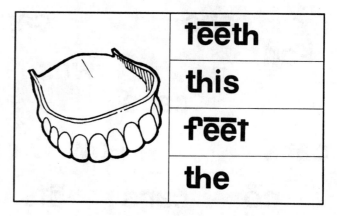

tēēth
this
fēēt
the

Printed in the United States of America.

shē sat in the lāke.

shē sat in the lāke.

e e e _ _	cāme
d _ _ _ _	fog
ē _ _ _ _	shē
w _ _ _ _	rōad
p _ _ _ _	mēan

~~will~~

will girl pot will

mē now will gō

āte will will

will will

will wāve fish will if will

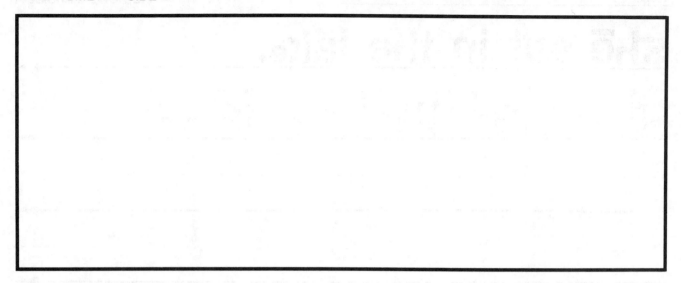

cat
girl
man
pot

rōad
gāte
lāke
dish

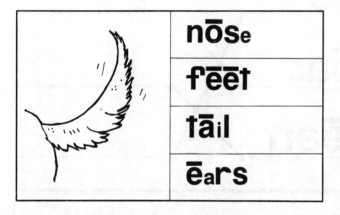

nōse
fēēt
tāil
ēars

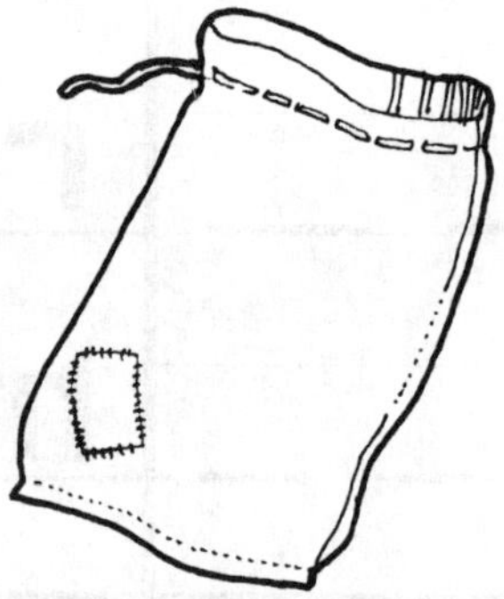

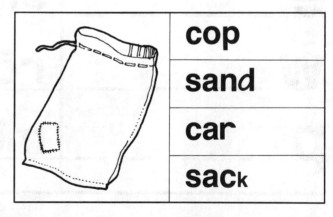

cop
sand
car
sack

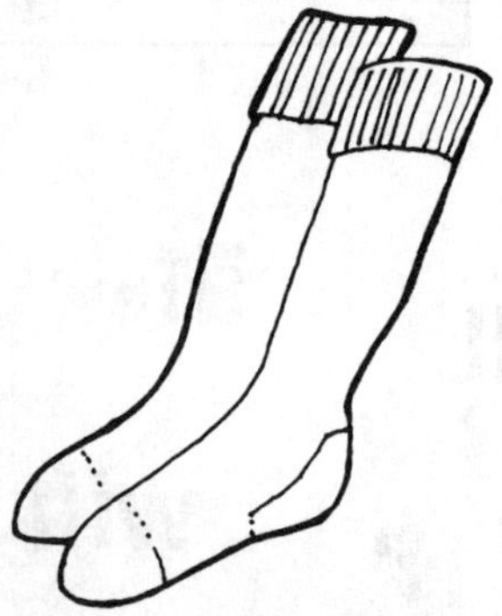

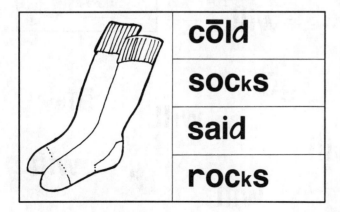

cōld
socks
said
rocks

rāke
cāke
cat
hōld

Printed in the United States of America.

NAME ____________________

the girl got wet.

~~girl~~

girl pots girl hōme girl girls said hug girl little has girl girl girl man girl nō girl

ron was in the rāin.
hē got wet.

1. ron was in the...
   - rat
   - rāin
   - sand

2. hē got...
   - fat
   - sick
   - wet

e

d

g

p

w

I

the man has a sack.

hē has a mitt.

sam is mad.

hē māde a fuss.

hē is in the sun.

it is in the mud.

the man is not fat.

hē āte a nut.

I am on the log.

wē will ēat fish.

hē is in a car.

hē has a fan.

a rat is on a rug.

hē sat on a rock.

wē have sand.

a girl has a gōat.

Printed in the United States of America.

the girl and the dog

the girl said, "I can tēach the dog to run."

the dog said, "nō."

the girl said, "I will tēach the dog to run."

the dog said, "nō. the girl can not tēach mē to run. I can run. ha ha."

Printed in the United States of America.

NAME ______________________

the girl got a cat.

~~went~~

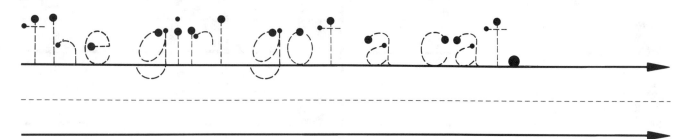

is went sō went sat went went went tēach nēēd now went was went went had sand went

the girl went to a shop.
shē got a cat.

1. the girl went to a...
   - ship
   - car
   - shop

2. shē got a...
   - cat
   - dog
   - car

d

e

p

n

s

r

that man is mēan.

hē āte a fig.

a man will ēat ham.

a girl has a sack.

the man has a cow.

hē is in the mud.

a girl has a fan.

a nut is on a log.

the girl can run.

hē has the māil.

shē has a pot.

wē will sit in sand.

shē ran and ran.

this cat is fat.

wē lock the nut.

a man is in a shack.

Printed in the United States of America.

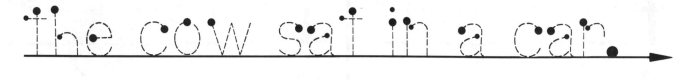

the cow sat in a car.

~~pet~~

pets sat pet wish pet pot

said pet gō pet pet dog

pet pet pet pet the nō

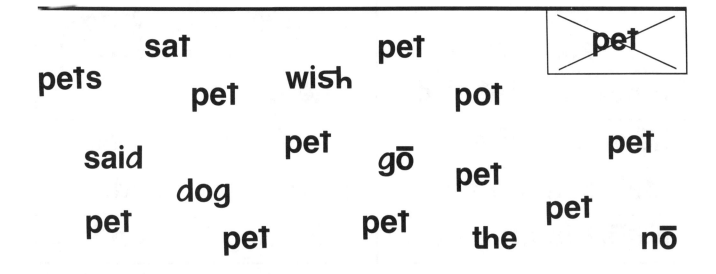

the cow was on the rōad.
the men got mad.

1. the cow was on the...
   - car
   - rōad
   - farm

2. the men got...
   - sad
   - māde
   - mad

t _ _ _ _ _ _ u _ _ _ _ _ _

d _ _ _ _ _ _ I _ _ _ _ _ _

p _ _ _ _ _ _ ch _ _ _ _ _

a cat has fat fēēt.

hē will ēat fish.

shē is in the mud.

a gōat is on a car.

hē has a pot.

a gōat āte a sock.

wē are not sad.

the dog is on a log.

his cat is fat.

shē has the māil.

hē has a shack.

sam āte cōrn.

this man is ōld.

his fēēt are wet.

shē is in a car.

that dog is mad.

Printed in the United States of America.

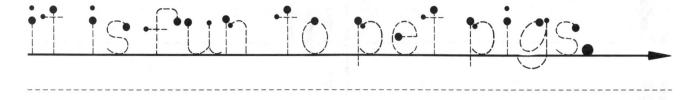

it is fun to pet pigs.

~~rōads~~

rōads will rōads rōads for shāve and rōads not rōads rōads car gōat rōads rōads āte rōad rōads

the gōat went to the park.

the girl went to the farm.

1. the gōat went...

- in a car
- in the rāin
- to the park

2. the girl went to the...

- car
- farm
- park

d ______ m ______

w ______ h ______

f ______ l ______

the pot has nō top.

shē will fēēd a pig.

shē sat in a lāke.

the fish has a hat.

wē are on a ship.

shē will ēat cōrn.

now I am cōld.

the man has socks.

the girl can run.

a cōat is in mud.

mom has a sock.

that is his dog.

his fēēt got hot.

shē is on a hill.

I will run.

hē sat on a gāte.

Printed in the United States of America.

NAME ______________________________

hē had a red nōse.

~~red~~ (nōse)

said red nōse cow

nōse red nōse hē

nōse rōad red

nōse red nōse red nō

red gōat red nōse fēēl nōse

the little dog had a red nōse.
hē was mad.

1. the little dog had a...
- big nōse
- hot nōse
- red nōse

2. hē was...
- sad
- mad
- big

b b b

ā

g

t

c

i

shē can kick.

I am not a fish.

the gōat āte a hat.

wē are in the rāin.

wē can gō in a car.

shē will kiss him.

hē has a big fish.

I fēēd the cat.

his ēars are little.

shē sat with a cat.

mom has a rāke.

hē will ēat cāke.

hē sat on a log.

the man has a cow.

shē has nō tēēth.

this rat is fat.

Printed in the United States of America.

NAME ______________________________

shē got a red hat.

do (crossed out)	nō (circled)

nō gāve
do nō do
gō
nō
and do the nō do
nō do
nō do
do on did nō was

the fish got a hat.
the cow got a car.

1. the fish got...
   - a hat
   - a gōat
   - a fish

2. the cow got a...
   - cat
   - car
   - cow

d ______

c ______

b ______

ē ______

g ______

r ______

a cow can lick mē.

the girl got wet.

hē has a hat.

I have cōrn.

wē will ēat cōrn.

I am not fat.

a man is on a rōad.

shē has socks.

hē has a gōat.

the girl is cōld.

shē ran in the sand.

that dog is mad.

a dog is in a car.

shē sat on a log.

that is a cop.

I can run.

Printed in the United States of America.

a girl and a gōat

a girl was on the rōad to a farm. shē met a gōat. shē said, "gō with mē to the farm. wē will pet a pig."

the gōat said, "I pet ducks and I pet chicks. I do not pet pigs."

the girl said, "it is fun to pet pigs. pigs are fat."

the gōat said, "I will not gō to the farm. I will gō to the park and pet a duck."

sō the gōat went to the park to pet a duck. and the girl went to the farm to pet a pig.

Printed in the United States of America.

the bug bit the log.

~~on~~	(sō)

on sō on is on sō pet sō rōad with sō on sō hit sō men on on on nō sō

the bug got mad.
sō shē bit a log.

1. the bug...
   - got big
   - got mad
   - got sad

2. sō shē bit a...
   - dog
   - lock
   - log

sh _____ _____ _____ _____

o _____ _____ _____ _____

b _____ _____ _____ _____

ā _____ _____ _____ _____

v _____ _____ _____ _____

p _____ _____ _____ _____

duck • 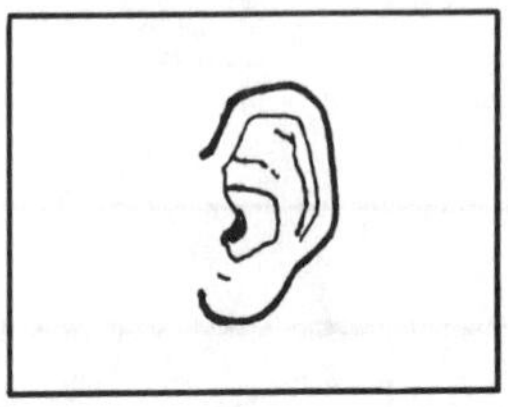

nōse • 

ēar • 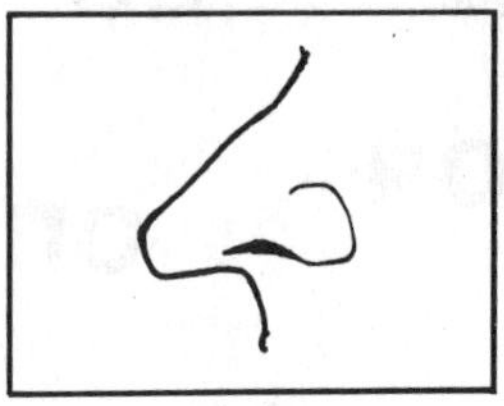

girl • 

shack • 

shēēp • 

pig • 

rug • 

cōat • 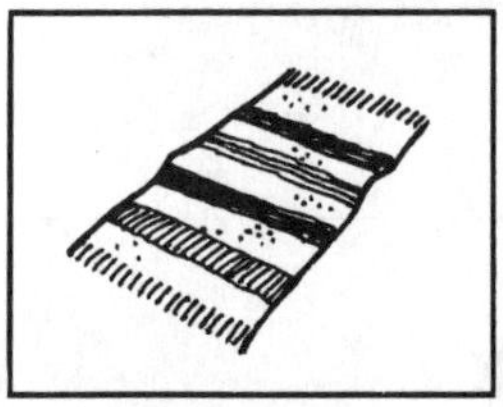

car • 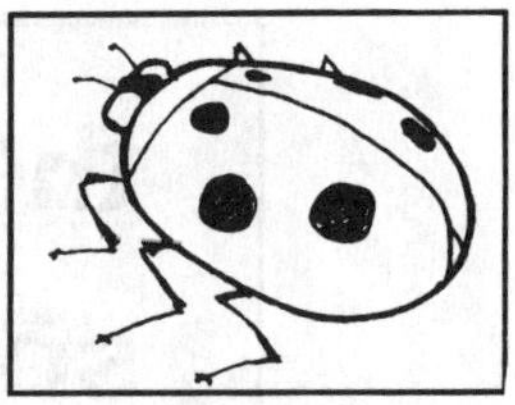

bug • 

cōrn • 

Printed in the United States of America.

NAME ______________________

shē āte the log.

~~big~~ (bug)

bug big in big car bug big fat big bug bug big big was bug bit big bug she cow bug

a big bug met a little bug.
hē said, "let's gō ēat."

1. a big bug met a little…

- big
- dog
- bug

2. hē said, "let's gō…"

- hōme
- ēat
- slēēp

I ______

ō ______

b ______

ch ______

k ______

h ______

dog

gāte

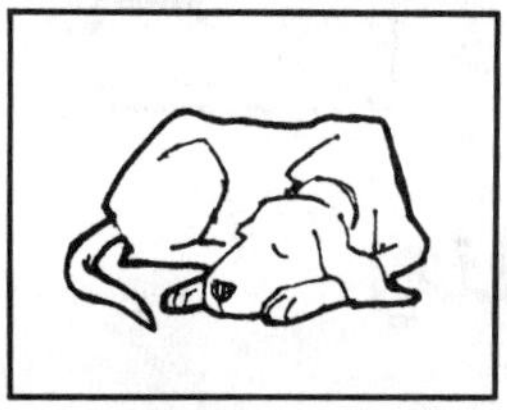

rōad

fēēt

ship

fish

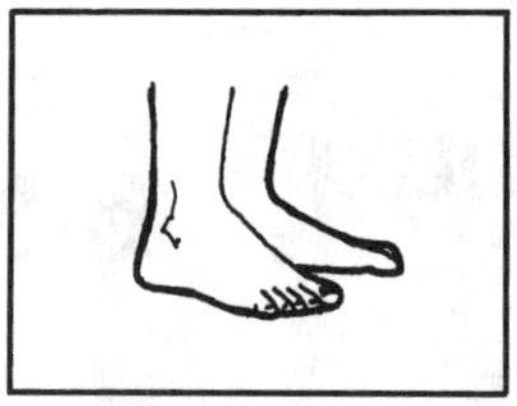

lāke

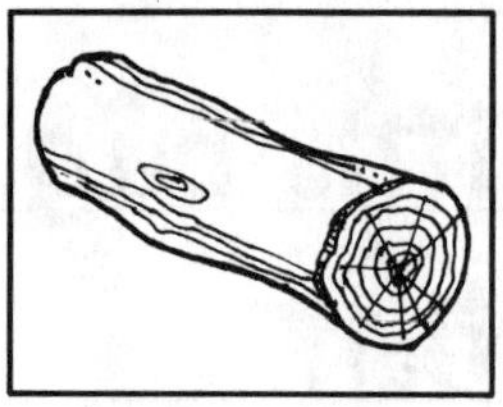

log

rāke

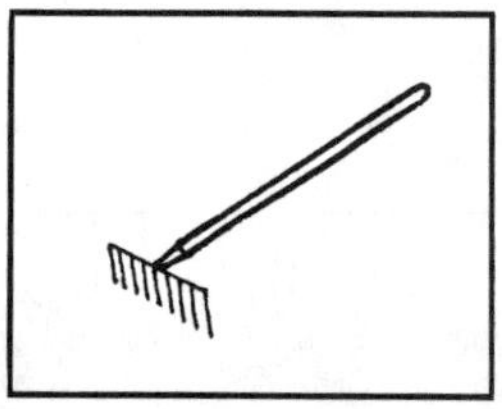

hat

gōat

cōrn

Printed in the United States of America.

The bug was on a dog.

get pet gāve get pet

get pet pot get pet get if get pet now pet sō get get nēēd get pet pet pet

the dog said, "I am a dog. I am not a bus."

1. the dog said, "I am a...

- log
- frog
- dog

2. I am not a..."

- bug
- bus
- bēē

b ___ ___ ___ ___ ___

e ___ ___ ___ ___ ___

ch ___ ___ ___

ē ___ ___ ___ ___

ī ī ī ___ ___ ___

th ___ ___ ___

tēēth 

sick 

tāil 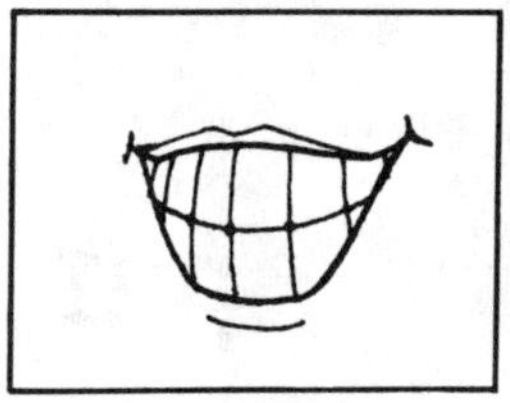

ēar 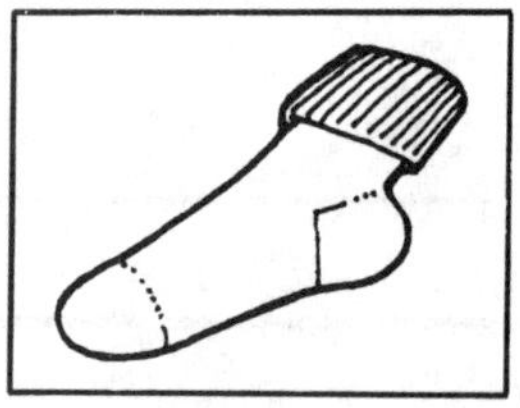

gāte 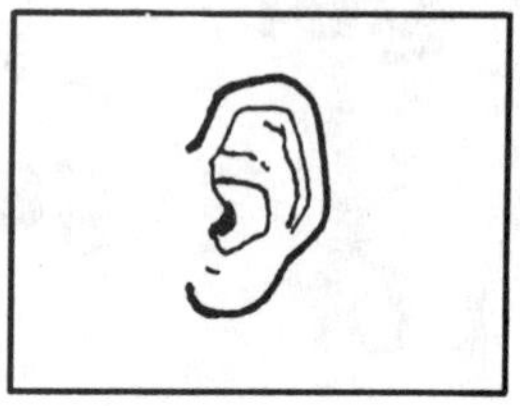

sock 

hē 

dish 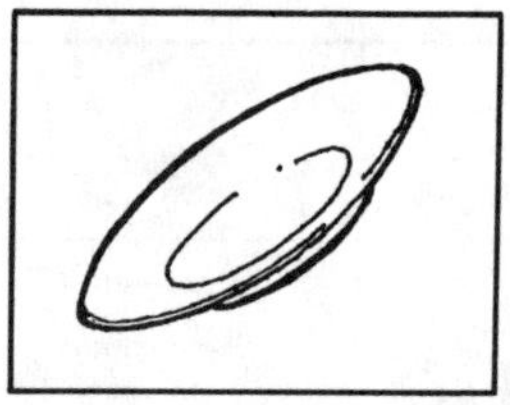

shē 

pigs 

logs 

fish 

Printed in the United States of America.

a man had a tub.

hāte ~~hāte~~ hat

hāte hat hot hat
sack hāte had hāte
hat hāte hat
hāte red hat
hat and hāte hat is hats hāte

the man had a tub.
hē said, "I lIke to rub, rub."

1. the man had a...
- tub
- top
- bug

2. hē said, "I lIke to..."
- run, run
- rēad, rēad
- rub, rub

ī

b

e

sh

p

g

gōat

sack

cat

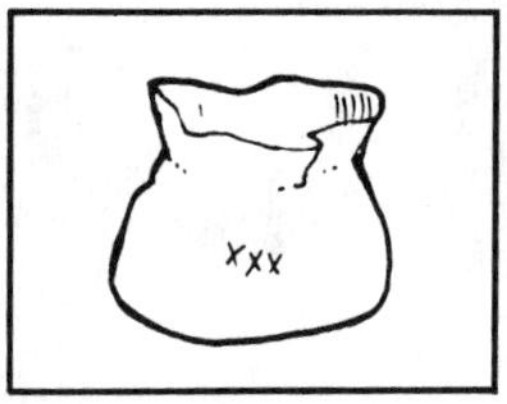

bug

nōse

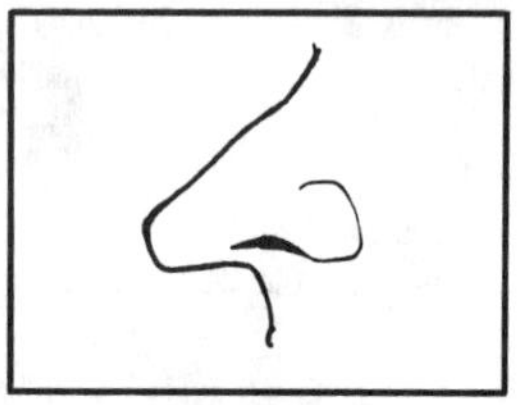

kitten

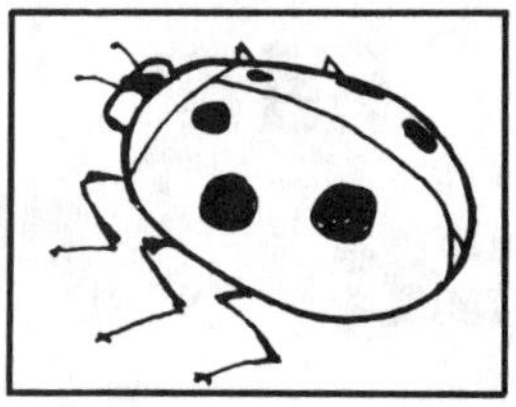

log

lock

car

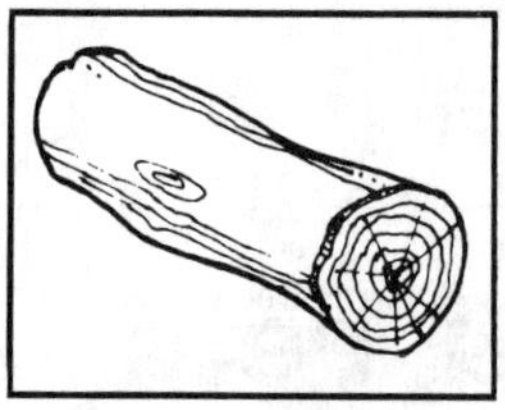

hat

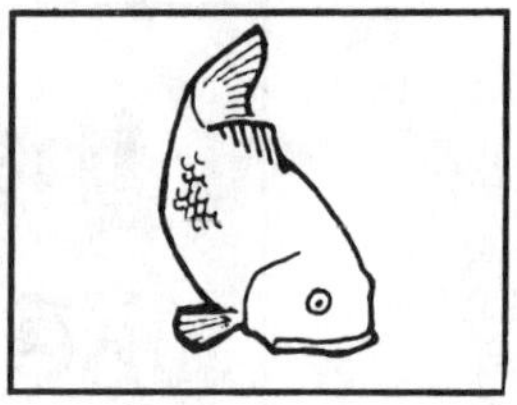

fish

duck

Printed in the United States of America.

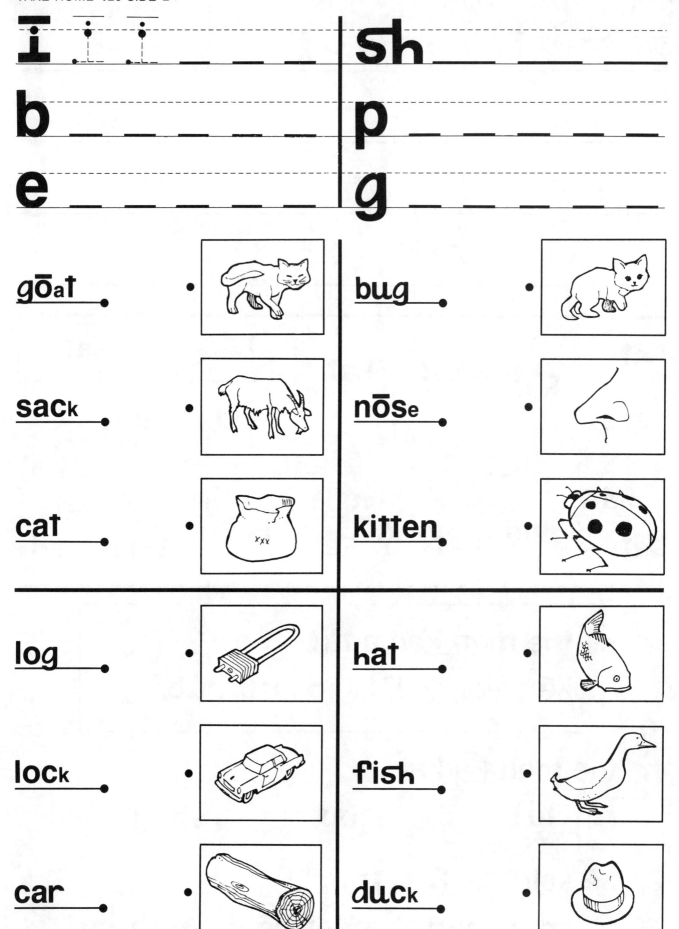

shē met a fat cat.

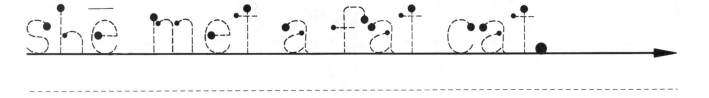

girl (crossed out)	talk (circled)

talk girl tāke girl

sō talk talk ship girl

girl got talk it girl

talk girl with girl talk talk walk

"can cats talk?" the girl said.

the cat said, "I can talk."

1. "can cats talk?" the...
   - man said
   - girl said
   - gōat said

2. the cat said, "I can..."
   - talk
   - run
   - wish

b ___ ___ ___ ___ ___ r ___ ___ ___ ___ ___

ch ___ ___ ___ ___ ī ī ī ___ ___ ___

f ___ ___ ___ ___ ___ l ___ ___ ___ ___ ___

lēaf ___ • 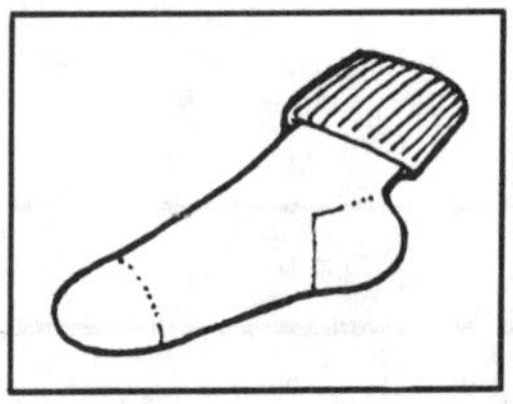

sock ___ • 

dog ___ • 

pig ___ • 

cōat ___ • 

shēēp ___ • 

tāil ___ • 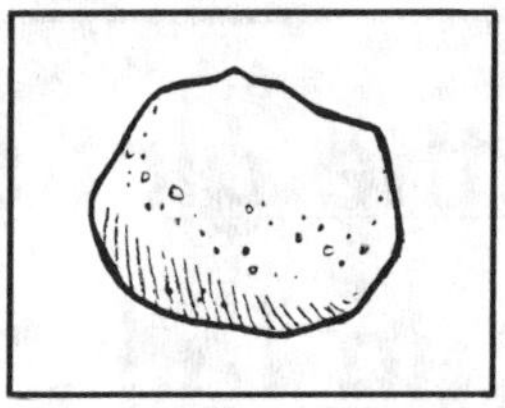

nōse ___ • 

rock ___ • 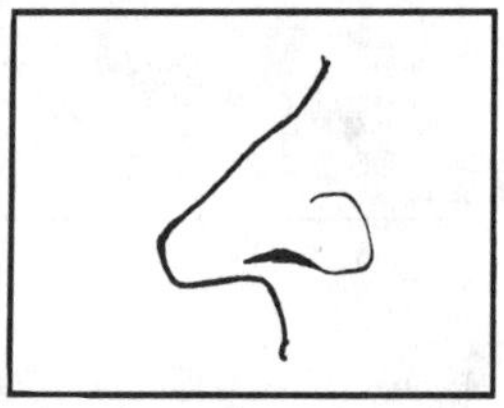

cōrn ___ • 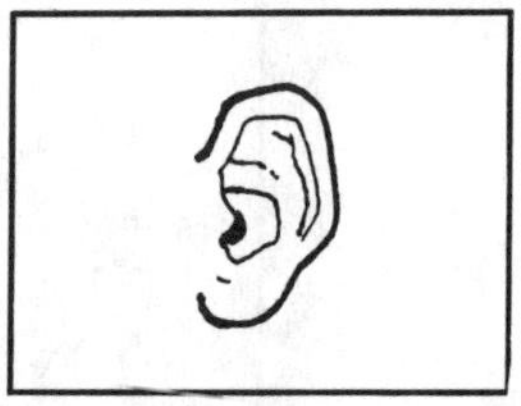

ēar ___ • 

lāke ___ • 

Printed in the United States of America.

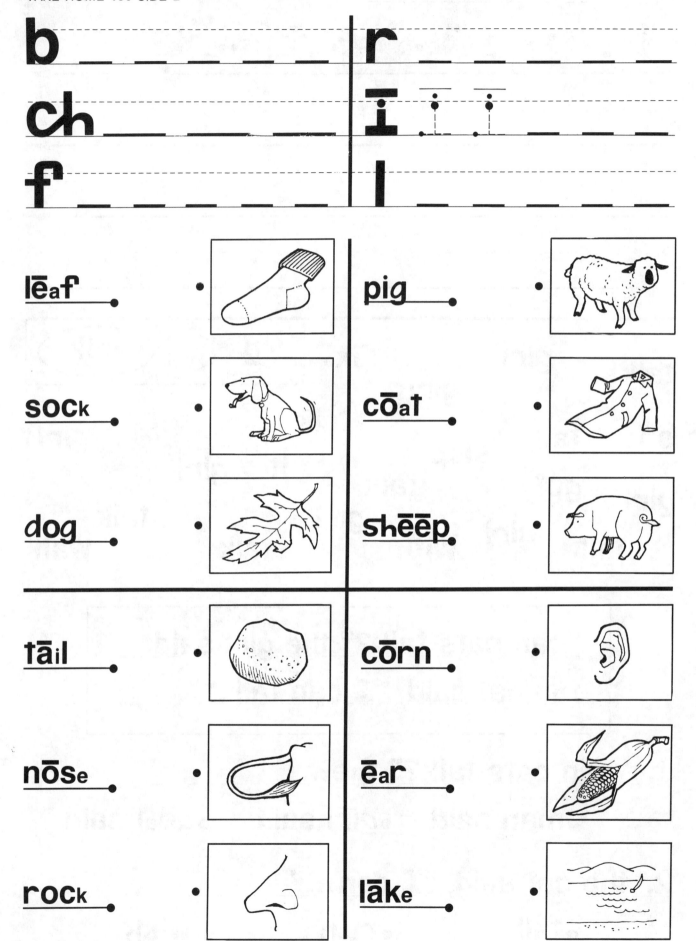

a bug and a dog

a bug and a dog sat on a log. the dog said, "that bug is sō little I can not sēē him on the log."

the bug said, "I am big."

the dog said, "that bug on the log is not big."

the bug said, "I will ēat this log." and hē did. hē bit and bit and bit at the log. the bug said, "now that dog can sēē how big I am."

the dog said, "that bug can ēat logs as well as a big bug."

Printed in the United States of America.

1. the girl got...

- ten fish
- five fish
- nō fish

2. did shē give fish to the dog?

- yes
- nō

3. the dog went...

- hōme
- to slēēp
- in the lāke

ī ___	l ___
I ___	c ___
sh ___	ā ___

a man had a car.
the car was red.

1. a man had a...

- card
- cat
- car

2. the car was...

- big
- red
- little

shē got fīve fish.

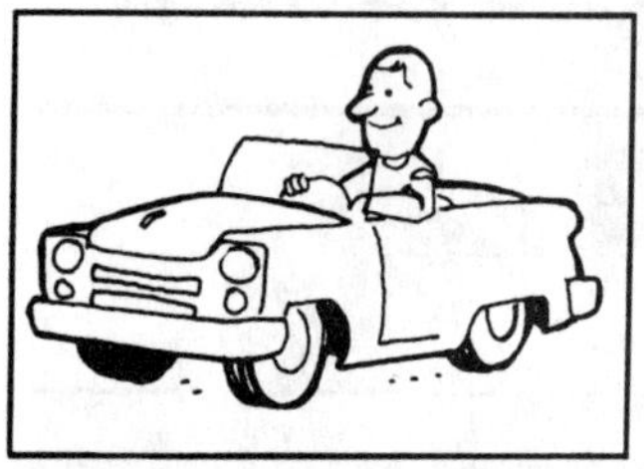

hē has a fan.

shē is sick.

the man is in a car.

wē āte cōrn.

the cat has big fēēt.

Printed in the United States of America.

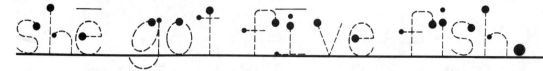

1. the rabbit went down on his...

- feet
- tail
- nose

2. the rat slid down on his...

- feet
- tail
- nose

3. the rat got a sore...

- nose
- hand
- tail

i ______	d ______
k ______	r ______
b ______	g ______

the girl went for a walk.
she met a fat pig.

1. the girl went for a...

- walk
- pig
- talk

2. she met a...

- fat pig
- little pig
- dog

hē slid on his nōse.

this man is mad.

a rat ran.

the girl can run.

the dog has big ēars.

shē has a rāke.

Printed in the United States of America.

1. the dog said, "pigs live…"

- on farms
- on ships
- in parks

2. the pig said, "I am a…"

- dog
- rich pig
- fat pig

3. the ship rocked and the dog…

- got wet
- was fat
- got sick

y y y ___ ___ ___	k ___ ___ ___ ___ ___
o ___ ___ ___ ___ ___	i ___ ___ ___ ___ ___
ī ___ ___ ___ ___ ___	b ___ ___ ___ ___ ___

a girl went fishing.
shē did not get fish.

1. a girl went…

- hōme
- running
- fishing

2. shē did not get…

- sick
- fish
- fans

I live on a ship.

hē sat on a log.

that dog has a hat.

shē fēēds the duck.

I am mad.

a little cat has fun.

Printed in the United States of America.

1. the dog dug a hōle in the...

- lāke
- cop
- yard

2. did the man get mad?

- yes
- nō

3. did the cop nēēd a cop dog?

- yes
- nō

ō _ _ _ _ _	k _ _ _ _ _
y y y _ _ _	ch _ _ _ _
o _ _ _ _ _	w _ _ _ _

a rat līkes to ēat.
hē ēats a red lēaf.

1. a rat līkes to...

- sit
- ēat
- run

2. hē ēats a...

- little lēaf
- fat lēaf
- red lēaf

The dog dug a hōle.

this fish is fat.

a dog sat on a rock.

wē are on a ship.

hē has a pot.

the gāte is big.

Printed in the United States of America.

NAME ________________________

1. ron said,...

- "nō"
- "not"
- "yes"

2. did ron pāint the bed red?

- yes
- nō

3. did ron pāint a car red?

- yes
- nō

n	y y y
h	u
k	m

a man went on a ship.
the ship was big.

1. a man went on a...

- hill
- ship
- cow

2. the ship was...

- big
- little
- red

ron got the pāint.

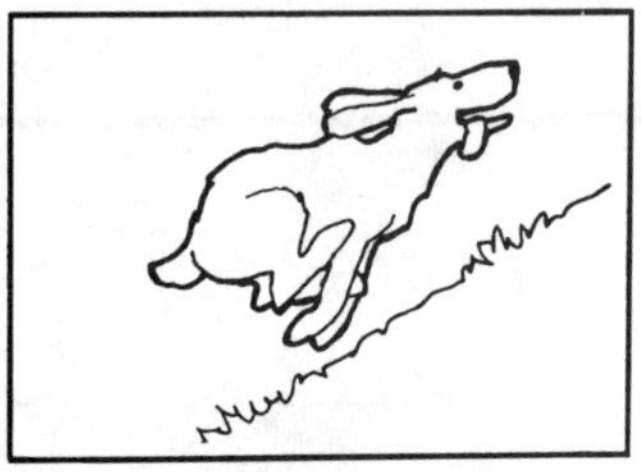

hē went to slēēp.

shē can kick.

a dog ran up a hill.

hē āte a lēaf.

this sock is big.

Printed in the United States of America.

the dog that āte fish

a girl went fishing with a dog. that dog āte fish. the girl did not līke the dog to ēat fish. "do not ēat the fish," shē said.

the girl went fishing and the dog went to slēēp. the girl got fīve fish.

"give mē the fīve fish," the dog said.

"nō," the girl said. "mōre fish are in the lāke. dīve in and get them."

sō the dog went in the lāke. and the girl went to slēēp.

the end

Printed in the United States of America.

NAME ____________________

1. the bōy said, "let's gō to..."

- the ship
- the park
- the farm

2. the bōy said, "wē nēēd a..."

- cat
- park
- car

3. did they rīde to the park?

- yes
- nō

c ___ ___ ___ ___ ___	f ___ ___ ___ ___ ___
o ___ ___ ___ ___ ___	s ___ ___ ___ ___ ___
ē ___ ___ ___ ___ ___	g ___ ___ ___ ___ ___

a dog dug a hōle.
a man fell in the hōle.

1. a dog dug a...

- hill
- hōle
- mōle

2. a man fell in the...

- lāke
- yard
- hōle

they ran to the park.

shē kissed him.

a duck can walk.

hē has a mitt.

this pot has nō top.

shē sat with a cat.

Printed in the United States of America.

1. ann and her dad went hunting for...

- rabbits
- pigs
- dēēr

2. did the girl fīnd a dēēr?

- yes
- nō

3. the girl did not get a pet...

- dog
- dēēr
- cat

d ____	o ____
a ____	g ____
b ____	p ____

a bōy had red pāint.
sō hē māde a car red.

1. a bōy had red...

- pigs
- pots
- pāint

2. sō hē māde a car...

- red
- run
- rōad

thē girl has pets.

a cow will lick him.

hē has nō socks.

this hat is big.

shē can dīve.

that man is fishing.

Printed in the United States of America.

NAME ______________________

1. a bōy sent a card to his...

- mother
- brother
- dad

2. the cop gāve the card to her...

- mother
- brother
- dad

3. a bōy said, "give mē that..."

- man
- card
- fish

p ____________	w ____________
e ____________	ā ____________
h ____________	ē ____________

a girl met a bōy.
shē said, "let's dig a hōle."

1. a girl met a...

- dog
- bōy
- pig

2. shē said, "let's..."

- sit
- run
- dig a hōle

hē gāve mom a card.

this bug is little.

shē fēēds the pig.

the gōat āte a can.

that cop was mad.

hē has a duck.

Printed in the United States of America.

hunting for a deer

ann said to her dad, "let's go find a deer for a pet."

so ann and her dad went hunting for a deer. a deer came up to them. ann said, "you can be a pet."

the deer said, "no, a deer is not a pet. dogs are pets. and cats are pets. I am not a pet. but I will let a girl and her dad pet me."

the girl said, "that will be fun."

and it was.

now, the girl has a pet dog and a pet cat. they go with her to hunt for the deer that she can pet.

the end

Printed in the United States of America.

NAME ______________________

1. a fat fox went in...

- a lāke
- a shop
- a box

2. did the fat fox hit the box?

- yes
- nō

3. the fox and his brother went...

- to sit
- to slēēp
- to slīde

ō _ _ _ _ _	d _ _ _ _ _
p _ _ _ _ _	h _ _ _ _ _
w _ _ _ _ _	x x x _ _

a boy had a toy.
the toy was red.

1. a boy had a...

- mother
- toy
- card

2. the toy was...

- a mother
- big
- red

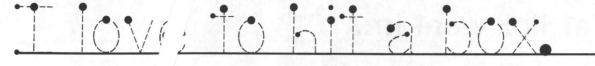

I love to hit a box.

this dog is mēan.

shē has socks.

a cow was on a rōad.

hē sat in a car.

a dog went to slēēp.

Printed in the United States of America.

1. the bug sat on the shōre of...

- a lāke
- a cāke
- a snāke

2. hē did not līke to get...

- fat
- shōre
- wet

3. hē did not have a...

- farm
- car
- hōme

x x x ___ ___ ___

p ___ ___ ___ ___ ___

o ___ ___ ___ ___ ___

k ___ ___ ___ ___ ___

c ___ ___ ___ ___ ___

b ___ ___ ___ ___ ___

a boy had a box.
a fox went in the box.

1. a boy had a...

- box
- fox
- car

2. a fox went in...

- a hōle
- the box
- a fox

a bug sat at the lake.

a man sat on a rock.

a rabbit āte a lēaf.

the cop had a dog.

shē will dīve.

a cat will lick her.

Printed in the United States of America.

1. a big ____ cāme and sat on the shōre.

   • rat • man • ēagle

2. the eagle said, "give mē a ____."

   • dīme • can • bug

3. did the bug give the eagle a dīme?

   • yes • nō

4. did the bug gō to the other sīde?

   • yes • nō

1. the m____ is fat.
2. hē has a f____.

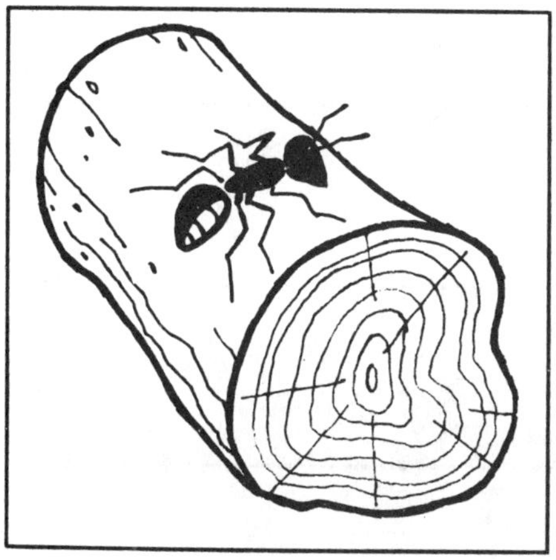

1. the bug is an a____.
2. the ant is on a l____.

a little bug bit a big bug.
the little bug was mad.

1. a little ____ bit a big bug.

- man
- bag
- bug

2. the little bug was ____.

- big
- mad
- red

e	ā
ch	x
th	y

hē sat on the shōre.

1. a bug and a ____ met on a rōad.

- pig
- man
- gōat

2. the bug bit a ____.

- dog
- log
- bug

3. the pig bit ____.

- his leg
- the bug
- a man

4. did the pig bīte better?

- yes
- nō

1. sh______ has a cat.

2. they are on a r______.

1. the m______ is at the lāke.

2. hē has a f______.

hē līked to ēat.

sō hē āte bēans and cāke.

1. hē ____ to ēat.

- hātes
- līked
- did not līke

2. sō hē āte bēans and ____.

- cōrn
- fish
- cāke

t ____ o ____

i ____ ī ____

e ____ n ____

"I bīte," a bug said.

Printed in the United States of America.

the other sīde of the lāke

a bug sat on the shōre of a big lāke. the bug said, "I nēēd to get to the other sīde of this big lāke."

but the bug did not līke to get wet. hē said, "I līke to slēēp and I līke to rīde in a car. but I do not līke to get wet."

the bug did not have a car and hē did not have a bed. sō hē sat and sat on the shōre of the lāke.

then a big ēagle cāme and sat down on the shōre. the ēagle said, "you are sitting on the shōre and you are sad."

the bug said, "yes. I am sad. I nēēd to get to the other sīde of the lāke. I will give you a dīme."

the ēagle said, "yes. give mē a dīme and I will tāke you to the other sīde." sō the bug gāve the ēagle a dīme and got on the ēagle. they went ōver the lāke.

the end

Printed in the United States of America.

1. a girl went to the shop with her ____.

- car
- cat
- dog

2. then they went to the ____.

- lāke
- park
- car

3. shē said, "you can not ____ to mē."

- talk
- walk
- sit

4. did the cat talk?

- yes
- nō

1. the c______ is sitting.

2. hē is on the b______.

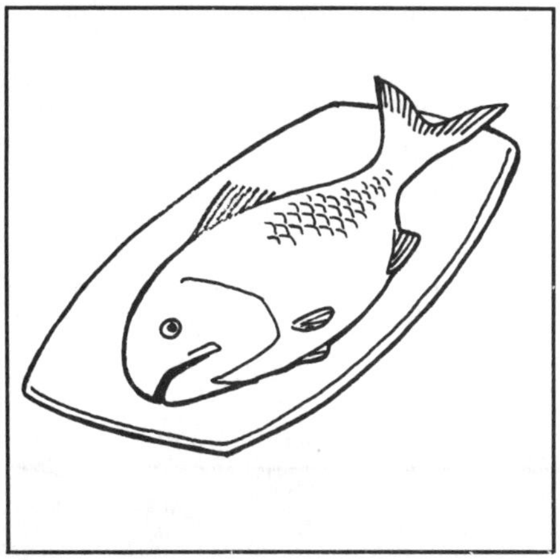

1. the f______ is not wet.

2. it is in the d______.

shē had a dog.

the dog did not talk.

1. shē had a ____.

- log
- bug
- dog

2. the ____ did not talk.

- fox
- dog
- bug

j
e
t
d
y
x

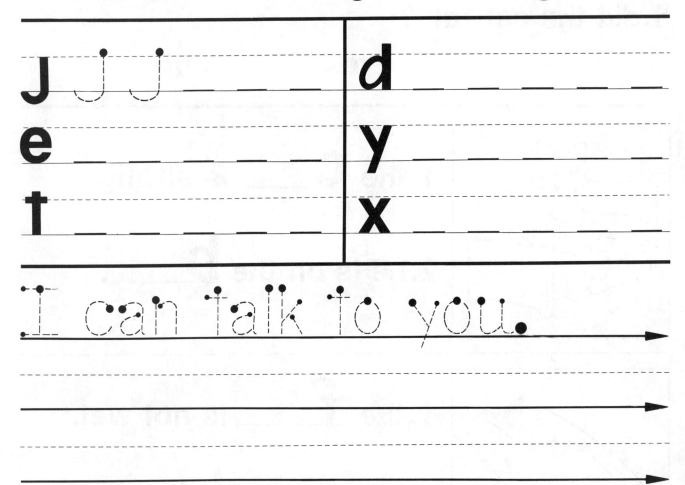

I can talk to you.

Printed in the United States of America.

NAME ______________________________

1. the girl said, "cats can not ____."

- talk
- walk
- slēēp

2. ann said, "can I have that ____?"

- can
- cat
- bug

3. the ____ said, "I will not gō with you."

- girl
- ann
- cat

4. ann said, "I will lēave this ____."

- park
- dark
- stōre

1. the man is a c______.

2. hē has a c______.

1. sh______ has a dog.

2. they are on a l______.

the man līked to swim.

sō hē jumped into the lāke.

1. the ____ līked to swim.

- boy
- man
- cow

2. sō hē ____ into the lāke.

- ran
- jumped
- fell

e

n

r

t

j j j

f

cats do not talk.

NAME ____________________

1. some girls went to the ____.

- shōre
- moon
- shop

2. a girl said, "I will fInd some ____."

- fun
- sun
- nuts

3. the moon cow said, "come with ____."

- you
- him
- mē

4. the ____ jumped into the pool.

- man
- boy
- cow

1. that d______ is slēēping.

2. hē is in b______.

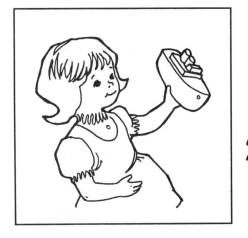

1. a toy is in her h________.

2. it is a toy sh________.

the man had a pet cow.

hē talked to the cow.

1. the man had a pet ____.

• cat • car • cow

2. hē ____ to the cow.

• ran • talked • walked

d ___ ___ ___ ___ ___ b ___ ___ ___ ___ ___

p ___ ___ ___ ___ ___ j j j ___ ___ ___

y ___ ___ ___ ___ ___ a ___ ___ ___ ___ ___

shē went to the moon.

1. the ōld car did not ____ .

• start • stop • shop

2. do rats have cars?

• yes • nō

3. did the big man start the car?

• yes • nō

4. the big man will kēēp sitting in ____ .

• the bus • the cāve • the car

1. a cat is on a p____ .

2. they are on a b____ .

1. a m____ is on the moon.

2. hē has a moon sh____ .

a girl went riding in a car.
shē went to a farm.

1. a girl went ____ in a car.

- riding
- talking
- walking

2. shē went to a ____.

- farm
- park
- shop

e	p
m	u
g	h

the car did not start.

Printed in the United States of America.

1. an ōld ____ was in the barn.

- dog
- car
- hōrse

2. a ____ said, "have you sēēn a hōrse?"

- man
- car
- cat

3. did the ōld man fīnd a hōrse?

- yes
- nō

4. did the ōld hōrse līke to gō fōr a rīde?

- yes
- nō

1. the man is f______.

2. his c______ is ōld.

1. a c______ is slēēping.

2. shē is on a l____.

a girl had a hōrse.

shē went rīding on a hōrse.

1. a ____ had a hōrse.

- man
- gōat
- girl

2. shē went rīding on a ____.

- hat
- hōrse
- gōat

u ___

p ___

j ___

o ___

y ___

e ___

they went riding.

Printed in the United States of America.

the cat that talked

a girl had a cat. shē loved her cat. shē talked to her cat.

then the cat talked to her. the girl said, "I must bē slēēping. cats can not talk."

the cat said, "you talk to mē. sō I can talk to you."

the girl gāve the cat a big hug. "I never had a cat that talked."

the cat said, "I never had a cat that talked ēither." the girl and the cat talked and talked.

then ann cāme to the park. shē went up to the girl and said, "can I have that cat?"

the cat said, "I will not gō with you."

ann said, "I must bē slēēping. cats do not talk. I will lēave this park." and shē did.

the end

Printed in the United States of America.

NAME ______________________________

1. bill līked to gō ____.

- riding
- fishing
- hunting

2. bill did not get ____.

- fish
- fat
- mad

3. bill had a ____ on his līne.

- bug
- rug
- tug

4. bill had an ōld ____.

- boy
- fish
- box

1. this dog is m______.

2. a bug bit his l______.

1. shē is h______.

2. shē has a f______.

a girl went fishing.
shē got fīve fish.

1. a girl went ____.

• walking • fishing • running

2. shē got ____ fish.

• fīve • nīne • nō

ȳ y y

p

r

s

b

c

bill did not get fish.

Printed in the United States of America.

NAME ____________________

1. did bill get fish?

- yes
- nō

2. the boys said, "you have an ōld ____."

- car
- box
- fox

3. bill said, "that box is filled with ____."

- fish
- boys
- gōld

4. bill was ____.

- not sad
- a bug
- gōld

1. the c______ is on a hōrse.

2. the hōrse has a h______

1. shē got a f______.

2. hē got a c______.

a man went in a sāil bōat.

hē had a lot of fun.

1. a man went in a ____.

- sāil bōat
- little bōat
- sāil gōat

2. hē had a lot ____.

- of bōats
- of fun
- of cows

ī a

o u

i e

"it is gōld," hē said.

Printed in the United States of America.

1. the ēagle said, "I līke to ____."

run • flȳ • fish

2. the hōrse said, "can you ____ mē to flȳ?"

• love • wish • tēach

3. did the hōrse flȳ to the top of a barn?

• • yes • nō

4. hē ran into the ____ of the barn.

• sīde • top • back

1. the man has a b______.

2. the bug is on his h______.

1. that c______ is slēēping.

2. shē is on a r______.

an ēagle līked to flȳ.
hē did not sit in a trēē.

1. an ēagle līked ____.

- to ēat
- to sit
- to flȳ

2. hē did not sit in ____.

- a trēē
- a park
- a bed

b

k

j

v

f

i

an ēagle līkes to flȳ.

1. did the hōrse flȳ to the top of a car?

• yes • nō

2. the hōrse ran into the ____ of the car.

• top • sīde • back

3. the hōrse ran with the ēagle on his ____.

• top • sīde • back

4. did they have fun?

• yes • nō

1. this dog is in a c________.

2. a c________ is on the car.

1. this p________ has fun.

2. hē is in the m________.

an ōld car did not run.

the girl got mad at the car.

1. an ōld ____ did not run.

- cat
- car
- cow

2. the girl got ____ at the car.

- bad
- sad
- mad

p

x

ȳ ȳ ȳ

h

k

j

the hōrse ran.

Printed in the United States of America.

1. shē brushed her tēēth ____ tīmes a dāy.

•nīne •six •nō

2. shē had a ____ tooth brush.

•toy •red •gōld

3. did her tēēth shīne līke the moon?

•yes •nō

4. did her mother have the tooth brush?

•yes •nō

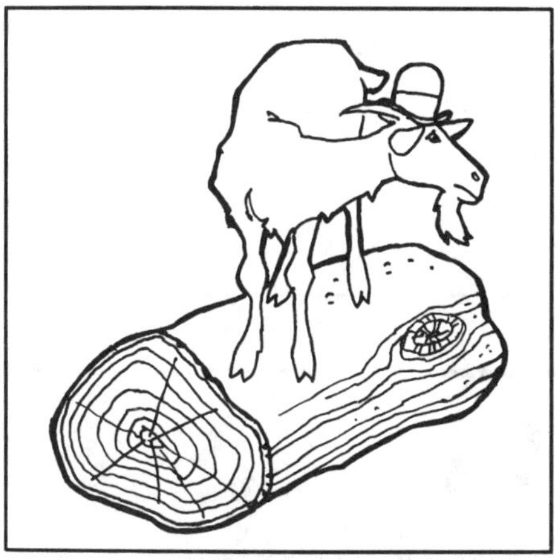

1. the gōat is on a l____.

2. hē has a h____.

1. this man is a c____.

2. hē is f____.

bill had a brush.
it was not a tooth brush.

1. bill had a ______.

- brush
- car
- bat

2. was it a tooth brush?

- yes
- nō

qu qu
c
b
d
f
g

I nēēd a tooth brush.

Printed in the United States of America.

an ōld hōrse and an ēagle

an ēagle was tēaching an ōld hōrse how to flȳ. but the ōld hōrse did not flȳ. the ōld hōrse ran into the sīde of a barn.

the ēagle said, "I will flȳ to the top of the car." and hē did.

but the ōld hōrse did not flȳ to the top of the car. hē ran into the sīde of the car. hē said, "mȳ mother and mȳ brother can not flȳ. I can not flȳ."

the ēagle said, "if you can not flȳ, you can not have fun."

the hōrse said, "I can run with an ēagle on mȳ back, and that is fun."

sō the ēagle sat on the back of the ōld hōrse and the ōld hōrse ran. "yes, this is fun," they said.

the end

Printed in the United States of America.

NAME ______________________________

1. the girl slipped on her ____.

- rug
- feet
- dog

2. the dog was brushing his ____.

- teeth
- nose
- feet

3. the dog had the red ____ brush.

- hand
- tooth
- nail

4. did the dog's teeth shine now?

- yes
- no

1. that bug is an a______.

2. it is on a c______.

1. she has a d______.

2. they are on the r______.

bill went to the park.

hē went in the big pool.

1. bill went to the ____.

- pond
- farm
- park

2. hē went in the ____ pool.

- bad
- big
- little

qu qu

x

k

ō

ā

ȳ ȳ ȳ

the girl smīled.

Printed in the United States of America.

1. an ēagle āte cāke and ham and ____.
   - nuts
   - cōrn
   - bēans

2. hē got ____.
   - fatter
   - better
   - sadder

3. a little eagle sat ____ a trēē.
   - on
   - under
   - at

4. then a ____ cāme hunting fōr ēagles.
   - man
   - boy
   - tīger

1. this c________ is slēēping.

2. shē is in b________.

1. the m________ is sitting.

2. hē is on a f________.

a girl līked to talk.
shē talked to the māil man.

1. a girl līked ____.

• to walk • to sit • to talk

2. shē talked to the ____.

• māil man • sad man • moon man

j z k y e r

a fat ēagle sat.

Printed in the United States of America.

NAME ______________________________

1. the fat ēagle cāme down on the ____.

- ēagle
- tīger
- hōrse

2. the ____ ran far awāy.

- ēagle
- tīger
- boy

3. do the ēagles māke fun of the fat ēagle?

- yes
- nō

4. they give him ____ and ham and cōrn.

- cans
- nuts
- cāke

1. this d______ runs.

2. shē has a h______.

1. the man is a c______.

2. his c______ is ōld.

a tīger sat under a trēē.
hē was looking fōr rabbits.

1. a tīger sat ___ a trēē.

- in
- nēar
- under

2. hē was looking fōr ___.

- girls
- rabbits
- pigs

z z z ___ ___ ___

n ___ ___ ___

f ___ ___ ___

e ___ ___ ___

u ___ ___ ___

r ___ ___ ___

they gāve him cāke.

Printed in the United States of America.

NAME ______________________

1. a man lIked to ____.

- sleep
- fish
- go fast

2. did he talk fast?

- yes
- no

3. the egg slipped and fell on his ____.

- head
- feet
- nose

4. the meat pie hit his ____.

- mother
- wife
- feet

1. that p______ is wet.

2. he is in the m______.

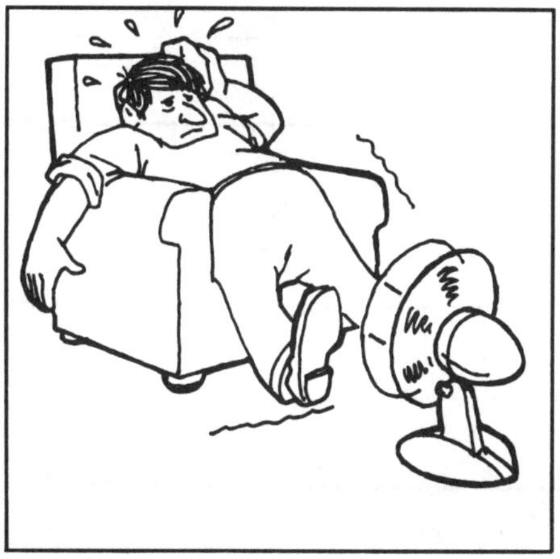

1. this man is h______.

2. he has a f______.

a girl walked down the rōad.

shē met a big fox.

1. a girl _____ down the rōad.

- looked
- walked
- ran

2. shē met a big _____.

- log
- fox
- dog

z z z	m
ū ū ū	n
b	r

hē āte a mēat pīe.

Printed in the United States of America.

1. the ____ said, "I will slōw down."

- mother
- wīfe
- man

2. sō hē did not gō ____ in his car.

- rīding
- fast
- slōw

3. did hē walk fast?

- yes
- nō

4. did hē ēat fast?

- yes
- nō

1. the m______ is at the lāke.

2. hē is on a l______.

1. that d______ is sitting.

2. shē is on a b______.

hē fell in the mud.

his nōse had mud on it.

1. hē ____ in the mud.

• walked • sat • fell

2. his ____ had mud on it.

• nōse • hat • fēēt

o

ū ū ū

f

k

t

g

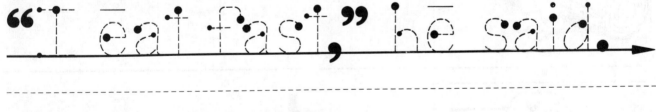

"I ēat fast," hē said.

Printed in the United States of America.

the fat ēagle

an ēagle līked to ēat. hē āte cāke and ham and cōrn. hē āte and āte, and hē got fatter and fatter. hē said, "I am sō fat that I can not flȳ."

hē sat in a trēē and the other ēagles māde fun of him. they said, "look at that fat, fat ēagle. hō, hō."

but then a tīger cāme hunting fōr ēagles. a little ēagle sat under a trēē. the tīger went after the little ēagle. the other ēagles yelled and yelled, but the little ēagle did not hēar them.

the fat, fat ēagle looked down and said, "I must sāve the little ēagle." sō hē jumped from the trēē. hē cāme down līke a fat rock on the tīger. and the tīger ran far awāy.

now the other ēagles do not māke fun of the fat, fat ēagle. they give him cāke and ham and cōrn.

this is the end.

Printed in the United States of America.